Praise for *It M.*

Samuel Whitefield has once again set a whole new standard for preaching and teaching what the Bible has to say on the topic of the "End Times." His new book *It Must Be Finished* is a wonderful treatment of a host of biblical texts that need to be read, understood, and taught afresh in these final days before our Lord returns. Readers will not be disappointed by this book nor will it treat this subject in a wearisome and hackneyed way: rather, it will produce a whole new set of understandings that unfortunately have all too often lain dormant in the church for far too long. I urge the church along with its pastors and teachers to quickly get a copy and begin the conversation and action demanded by our Lord to meet the coming days of the End Times.

Dr. Walter C. Kaiser, Jr., President Emeritus, Gordon-Conwell Theological Seminary

Samuel Whitefield has successfully anchored the story and the message of the "end times" within the larger story of God's glorious plan of redemption. Sadly, far too many Christians feel as though the subjects of the return of Jesus and the end times are too confusing, because they've never understood the larger story of the Bible itself. By following the consistent threads of God's covenants, promises, and plans, Samuel has made the conclusion of the narrative and its profound implications so much easier to grasp. The closer we get to the end of the tale that we find ourselves in, the more important it is that we understand it. This book will greatly help any Christian who desires, not only to understand the broader biblical message, but also to fulfill their role within that story as it unfolds. I cannot more highly recommend *It Must Be Finished*.

Joel Richardson, *New York Times* best-selling author, speaker, and filmmaker

It Must be Finished is a strong and insightful read that will stir and inspire your heart for the return of Jesus Christ. Samuel has a way of "connecting the dots" in the mind of the reader about God's grand story line while simultaneously stirring vision for the church in the coming days. With so much hypothesis and speculation about the end times being propagated in our generation, it is refreshing to have a book like this that helps to anchor our hearts in the Word of God while equipping us to mentor and disciple others in these things.

Jim Stern, Lead Pastor, Destiny Church, St. Louis

Samuel Whitefield is proving to be a very capable theological thinker. It is wonderful to add him to the ranks of those who interpret the Bible in a straight forward manner according to the original context and literary genre. May God speed the acceptance of this book and its influence.

Dr. Daniel Juster, Author and Founder, Tikkun International

God is raising up "Shepherds according to His heart who will feed people on knowledge and understanding" so that hearts will be strengthened and minds will have clarity to understand what God is doing in the earth in these days. Samuel Whitefield is one of the shepherds who God is using to bring understanding of His heart and plans. The subject of the end times is so much more than graphs, charts, and timelines. It is ultimately a story, and when your heart connects to this story it causes faith, hope, and love to explode in your heart and mind. I've known Samuel Whitefield for ten years, and I can attest to his tireless labor to see the subject of the end times go from a topic only scholars understand to a subject the whole body of Christ can engage with.

Corey Russell, Senior Leadership Team, International House of Prayer of Kansas City, MO

Samuel Whitefield has been studying the Scriptures relating to the end times for many years now, praying for insight and digging deep into the plain sense of the text. In doing so, he challenges us to dive into these texts with him, also challenging us to ask: How does this apply to me today? You will be stirred and sobered and encouraged as you study along with Samuel.

Dr. Michael L. Brown, President, FIRE School of Ministry; author; speaker; and host of *The Line of Fire* broadcast.

Once again Samuel has written passionately and plainly about Jesus' grand redemptive plan for Israel and the nations which climaxed on

Calvary and will culminate with Jesus' second coming. In this book, Samuel helps readers navigate redemptive history with a clear meta-narrative undergirded by biblical reasons for Jesus' coming. It Must Be Finished is refreshing and helpful to anyone who desires to understand biblical eschatology and missiology.

Daniel Lim, Director, Center for Biblical End-Time Studies; CEO, International House of Prayer of Kansas City, MO

IT MUST BE FINISHED
MAKING SENSE OF THE RETURN OF JESUS

For Curt Freudenberger,

Ps 27:4

SAMUEL WHITEFIELD

ONE
KING
PUBLISHING

It Must Be Finished—Making Sense of the Return of Jesus
By Samuel Whitefield

Published by OneKing Publishing
PO Box 375
Grandview, MO 64030

Email: contact@oneking.global
Web: https://oneking.global

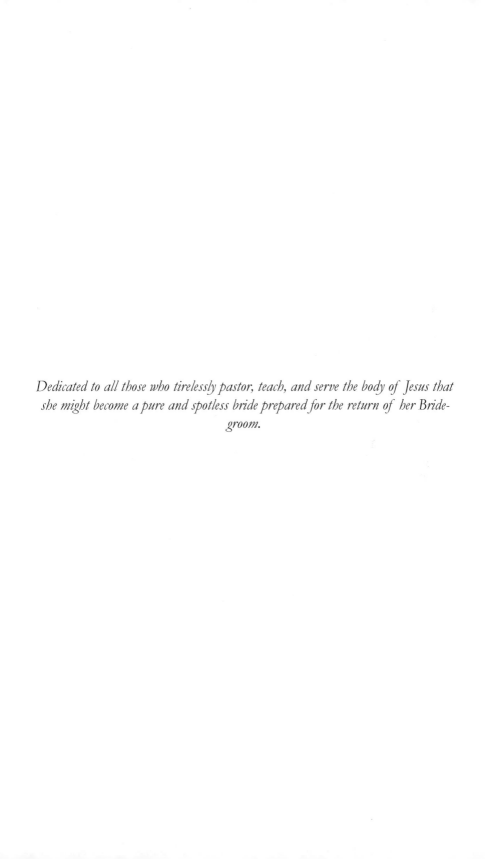

Dedicated to all those who tirelessly pastor, teach, and serve the body of Jesus that she might become a pure and spotless bride prepared for the return of her Bridegroom.

Contents

INTRODUCTION

When Jesus died on the cross, He cried out, "It is finished!"[1] In His death, Jesus did what previously seemed to be impossible. He secured the redemption of humanity and of the cosmos. Perhaps because of Jesus' well-known phrase, many people assume the cross fulfilled all of God's promises, but this is not what the Bible teaches.

Biblically speaking, the cross did not fulfill all the promises of God—it secured them.

Tragically, we have neglected much of what the Bible says about the fulfillment of God's promises. However, the full magnitude of what the cross accomplished is revealed in both what was fulfilled when Jesus died and what will be fulfilled in the events we refer to as the "end times."

God has staked His honor on His ability to fulfill specific promises, and the plan of redemption is not completed until these promises are fulfilled. According to Paul, we cannot even imagine what is coming with the fulfillment of all God's promises:

> *But, as it is written, "What no eye has seen, nor ear heard, nor the heart of man imagined, what God has prepared for those who love him." (1 Corinthians 2:9)*

The atonement was finished at the cross, but there is more to the story. *It must be finished.*

God Is Deeply Involved in History

History is not aimless. The Bible tells us God is deeply involved in human history. He is leading humanity, from generation to generation,

---

[1] John 19:30.

through a redemptive narrative towards a predetermined conclusion. *God is a master storyteller, and the plan of redemption is the most masterful story ever created.* Like all great stories, it climaxes at the end, but the end—what we call the "end times"—can become a confusing subject if you do not understand the overarching story. However, when you grasp the story of redemption through the lens of key promises and covenants, the end times become a glorious conclusion to God's plan in this age.

The notable men and women of the Bible were motivated to deep sacrifice and heroic faith by their longing for the day when God fulfills His promises and concludes the story. *The Bible's prediction of the end of the story should have the same effect on us as it did the saints who have gone before.* It is the hope set before us, but far too often we fail to live with a biblical hope and expectation of the end because we are disconnected from the story.

Like any good story, the end is the most important part; however, many find the end difficult to grasp. The reason is typically because we may know individuals and events in the Bible, but we struggle to connect them to the main elements that are driving the biblical story. *When we do not understand the key elements of the story, the end becomes confusing.* However, when we grasp the main elements of the story, the end is simply the logical conclusion of the story and to fully grasp the gospel we need to understand the end of the story.

Many people assume the cross fulfilled all of God's promises, but this is not true. *The cross secured all of God's promises, but it did not fulfill them all.* Therefore, to understand what is coming and to recognize God's activity in the earth, we need to know what He has set into motion that He must bring to completion. God's promises and covenants are the main elements of the story driving history towards His conclusion. When we recognize how they drive history we can better understand God's redemptive work and the role we play in the unfolding of the story.

An Unprecedented Moment

We live in an unprecedented moment in human history. *We live in the first possible generation that could give witness of the gospel to every tribe, nation, and tongue.* Fifty years ago, we did not know how many people groups lived in the earth much less where they were all located. At the time of this writing, we now know where every people group lives, and church leaders are beginning to strategically focus on reaching each one of them. There is no guarantee the mission will be fulfilled in our generation, but for the first time in human history, it is possible. This is an incredible milestone because the Bible predicts this witness must be given before the end will come.[2]

Additionally, we live in the first generation in human history where Israel has become a global controversy. Although Israel was always a central figure in the biblical narrative, during biblical times the vast majority of the earth was not even aware Israel existed. Today, for the first time in history, Israel has become a global issue affecting the nations.

This global focus on Israel, and particularly Jerusalem, does not make sense according to human logic. Jerusalem is not a center of world finance or global business. It does not produce natural resources that drive the global economy. There are far greater humanitarian challenges in the earth than Israel's complex relationship with the Palestinians. Though the issues surrounding Israel are important, there are much bigger conflicts in the earth. These other conflicts only receive a fraction of the attention Israel receives.[3] The global focus on Israel simply does not make sense apart from what the Bible says about a final conflict over the salvation of Israel.

Living in a time when either of these events were occurring would be momentous in and of itself, but we live in a time when both events are occurring simultaneously for the first time in history. This is unparalleled and unprecedented. While we must avoid unbiblical attempts to predict the return of Jesus, the New Testament instructs us to understand the times and seasons in the earth.[4] *Therefore, as we see the times and*

---

[2] See Matthew 24:14; 28:19; Acts 1:6–8; Revelation 5:9; 7:9.

[3] For example, in 2017 the United Nations (UN) adopted twenty resolutions on Israel and six on the rest of the world. In 2016 the UN also adopted twenty resolutions on Israel and six on the rest of the world, and in 2015 it adopted twenty resolutions on Israel and three on the rest of the world. See UN Watch. https://www.unwatch.org/2017-unga-resolutions-singling-israel/, https://www.unwatch.org/unga-adopts-20-resolutions-israel-4-rest-world-combined/, https://www.unwatch.org/un-to-adopt-20-resolutions-against-israel-3-on-rest-of-the-world/ (Accessed December 15, 2017).

[4] See Matthew 24:32–33; 1 Thessalonians 5:1–6.

seasons shifting, we want to understand God's redemptive plan so that we can recognize His activity in the earth and fully engage in His mission.

The Story—The Key to the End

We cannot understand the end times by only focusing on the end times. That is like trying to understand a movie by only watching the final ten minutes. *The key to understanding the main themes of the end times is to know the foundations of the biblical story and how they set up the end of the story.*

When you watch a movie, the end of the movie is the logical conclusion to the story. It may contain a few surprises, but the ending makes sense if you understood the beginning of the movie. The story prepares you for the dramatic conclusion. In the same way, the conclusion makes sense of everything that has gone before. In a way, the conclusion is the most critical part of the film because it resolves the conflict and reveals, perhaps, what the entire story has been about. The same is true of redemptive history.

Too often, the end times seem confusing and strange because we do not understand the redemptive story—the biblical story. Therefore, it's critical for us to see the end times as the logical conclusion to that story. We need to know the story of God's redemptive plan and how He advances His plan through key events in history.

Different views of the end times have led to many books being written on the subject, but the majority of these books describe end-time details without connecting them to the redemptive story. The result is that many believers have heard descriptions of end-time events but have very little understanding of why these events must happen and what role they play in the redemptive story. *Understanding how the events of the end times relate to the story of the Bible is required to fully comprehend the return of Jesus.*

The return of Jesus can seem complex and complicated when we do not understand how it is connected to the biblical story. Because some believers do not understand the story, they avoid the subject of Jesus' return altogether, even though Jesus' return is a core component of the gospel. Other believers approach the end times primarily as a puzzle and become so lost in the details of the end of the age that they focus more on charts and graphs than how the end times relate to the mission of God happening now. The answer in each case is to anchor the return of Jesus in the overarching story of the Bible by putting end-time events in the context of the biblical story.

When we fail to see Jesus' return as part of the biblical story, the end times become a subject that is more trivial than missional. However, the Bible is written as an unfolding story, a great drama, that is building in intensity, where each part of the story leads to the next and the details of that drama are given to provoke us to participate in God's mission. We are invited to join God in the resolution of His redemptive plan, and therefore, the church cannot fully understand its role without understanding His story.

Books written on the details of the end times are helpful, but it's not enough to know what happens in the future; we need to know what is propelling those specific events and why this age must conclude the way it will. *We must connect the main themes of the beginning of the biblical story and discover how they set up the end of the story.* That is what we will do in this book.

The Old Testament Sets the Stage

One of the most important parts of comprehending the plan of God is the way we perceive the Old Testament. Many believers think the Old Testament has been done away with, but the reality is not that simple. The Old Testament was the Bible the apostles preached from. *Our ability to fully grasp the redemptive story depends on our knowledge and understanding of the promises and foundations of the Old Testament.* Once we understand those foundations, we need to know how Jesus fulfills God's redemptive plan, how we are to live in light of what has been fulfilled, and what remains to be fulfilled.

When we study the Bible, or hear sermons on Sunday, we tend to spend most of our time on Paul, then study Jesus, and very rarely study the Old Testament. When we do hear messages based on Old Testament passages, it is usually to illustrate a New Testament truth or to serve as the subject of a topical sermon. Although Paul's letters to the churches are very practical and key for New Testament Christianity, he and the other New Testament authors assumed their audience had a solid foundation in the Old Testament that most modern believers are missing. As a result, many believers have become familiar with the language of Paul, and some of the story of Jesus, but do not understand the majority of Scripture.[5]

The Old Testament is the foundation of the redemptive story. While portions of it have been fulfilled, its key promises remain unfulfilled and continue to undergird the redemptive plan in our day. *God's promises are not only part of the past, they are part of our future.* To understand the story of God, then, we have to study the plan of God in its natural order. This means understanding the foundation of the Old Testament, the work of Jesus in His first and second coming, and finally how that is applied in a New Testament context.

When we learn the story in the right sequence, the plan of God becomes much easier to understand. In this book, we will make the foundations of the Old Testament straightforward and show how they continue to drive the redemptive story.

The coming of Jesus was a radical part of God's story, but it did not replace what God had begun. Jesus' coming did not replace the Old Testament promises; it secured them. Rather than redefining God's mission, Jesus' coming expanded it in a way that no one anticipated. As we will soon see, the promises spoken will still be fulfilled, but they will be fulfilled in a way that is far beyond anything we could ever imagine.

An Overview of Each Section

Before we jump headlong into the main text, here is a quick overview of each part of this book to help you see where we are going:

- In "Part 1: Why Study Jesus' Return," we look at the importance of studying the return of Jesus.

- In "Part 2: The Promises That Must Be Fulfilled," we will review the key promises of the Old Testament that have not yet been fulfilled but must be fulfilled. Jesus' first coming secured these promises but did not fulfill them. His second coming must fulfill them.

- In "Part 3: What Must Be Resolved—The Crisis of the Covenant," we concentrate on the crisis created by the Mosaic covenant regarding the fulfillment of the promises and how the

---

[5] Based on the number of words in the original languages, the Old Testament is about 77 percent of the Bible.

crisis continues to affect the nations to this day. We will examine how the first and second comings of Jesus are necessary to resolve finally and permanently the crisis of the Mosaic covenant so that the promises can be fulfilled.

- In "Part 4: God's Plan for the Nations," we will examine what the Bible says about the nations and how the promise made to Abraham about the nations will be fulfilled in a victorious end-time church.

- In "Part 5: The End-Time Conflict—War Over the Promises," we will examine how the fulfillment of God's promises sets the stage for the end-time conflict. We will also examine why Israel is so central in end-time events and how the nations are connected to those events. Finally, we will look at how understanding the end times is a missional issue for the church, not simply a theological one.

Part 1: Why Study Jesus' Return?

TWO PRIMARY REASONS TO STUDY JESUS' RETURN

Many believers never study the return of Jesus and the end times. There are a number of reasons for this. In some cases, it is because people simply have never given significant time to studying the subject. Others have heard teaching about Jesus' return or the end times that made the subject seem difficult and confusing. Still other believers avoid the subject because they have seen others engage in the subject in unbiblical ways. These include trying to determine the exact day of Jesus' return, focusing on escaping end-time events instead of building the church, and making premature predictions about things like the identity of the Antichrist.

While we want to avoid these mistakes, only a relatively small number of believers in history have made such mistakes, and their error should not keep us from the benefits of knowing what the Bible says about Jesus and His return. *The challenge of studying the return of Jesus is not the subject itself; it is how we respond to the subject.*

The proper response to the study of the end times is to grow in love for Jesus and become more engaged in His mission in the nations. The apostles in the New Testament taught about the return of Jesus, and it motivated them to build the church. It should do the same thing for us.

The study of the return of Jesus should result in three responses:

- *We love Jesus more and see Him as our ultimate hope.* If we live in peace or prosperity, studying the return of Jesus helps to keep us from placing our ultimate hope on our temporary prosperity. If we live in lack or suffering, the return of Jesus is a source of hope and encouragement in the midst of our trials.

- *We prepare ourselves to resist the most evil man in history.* Because the global church faces a number of wicked men in every generation, this preparation serves the church well. We resist by choosing to live holy lives rather than being seduced by evil and being willing to endure persecution even unto death.

- *Because we long for Jesus' return, we engage in God's mission.* The Bible gives us several things that will happen in the earth before the return of Jesus and then instructs us to labor for these things to come to pass. The desire for Jesus' return should cause us to become more involved in God's activity in the church.

Let's begin with two primary reasons we should study and understand the return of Jesus.

We Love Jesus

The first reason to study end times is because we love Jesus. When many people think about the return of Jesus, they think mostly about the Antichrist or the "great tribulation." Neither of these is the primary focus of the end times in the Bible. *The primary focus of the return of Jesus is Jesus.* Therefore, we cannot study or understand the end times correctly unless we keep Jesus central.

John made this point in Revelation 1:

> *The revelation of Jesus Christ, which God gave him to show to his servants the things that must soon take place. He made it known by sending his angel to his servant John. (v. 1)*

When John wrote the book of Revelation, he introduced it as, "The revelation of Jesus." John's book about the end times is not primarily about the Antichrist or great tribulation. It is primarily about Jesus. This was central in John's thinking, it is central in the Father's thinking, and it should be central in our thinking.

John told us the Father gave Jesus this grand story of events so that He could share it with His people. *From the Father's perspective, the end times are a gift to Jesus because they set the stage for His glory.* The Father reveals end-time information because He wants to invite the church, as the people who belong to Jesus, into the story He has planned to glorify His Son Jesus.

To emphasize the point, John also described his encounter with Jesus in Revelation 1:

> *I was in the Spirit on the Lord's day, and I heard behind me a loud voice. . . . Then I turned to see the voice that was speaking to me, and on turning I saw seven golden lampstands, and in the midst of the lampstands one like a son of man, clothed with a long robe and with a golden sash around his chest. The hairs of his head were white, like white wool, like snow. His eyes were like a flame of fire, his feet were like burnished bronze, refined in a furnace, and his voice was like the roar of many waters. In his right hand he held seven stars, from his mouth came a sharp two-edged sword, and his face was like the sun shining in full strength. When I saw him, I fell at his feet as though dead. But he laid his right hand on me, saying, "Fear not, I am the first and the last, and the living one. I died, and behold I am alive forevermore, and I have the keys of Death and Hades." (vv. 10, 12–18)*

John's encounter with Jesus is stunning when we remember John's life. John was the disciple who was probably the most familiar with Jesus. He referred to himself as the disciple Jesus loved.[1] When the disciples ate the Last Supper, John reclined right next to Jesus.[2] When Jesus warned someone would betray Him, the other apostles asked John to ask Jesus who it was.[3] John knew Jesus extremely well. In the Gospels, John was confident enough to sit next to Jesus and ask Him the questions other disciples were too afraid to ask.

However, when John encountered Jesus on the island of Patmos, he fell at His feet as though dead. Though John was very familiar with Jesus, in Revelation 1, he encountered Jesus in a way he had not known Him before. It left John shocked and stunned. All at once Jesus was both familiar and radically different from anything John had experienced before.

When Jesus came the first time, He refused to promote Himself.[4] Instead, He found great joy in speaking about God as Father.[5] When

---

[1] See John 13:23; 19:26; 20:2; 21:7, 20.

[2] See John 13:23.

[3] See John 13:23–25.

[4] See John 7:18; 8:49, 50.

[5] See Matthew 6:9; 10:29–31; John 1:18; 17:11, 24–26.

Jesus came, He revealed a part of the Father that was radically different from what the people had known of the God of Israel. What they knew was true, but it was incomplete. There was much more to God than what they had experienced at Sinai. He was the uncreated God, but He was also a tender Father.

 What Jesus did for the Father in His first coming is what the Father will do for Jesus in Jesus' second coming. The Father greatly desires to speak to the nations about His Son. He wants us to know what He knows about His Son. Just as ancient Israel knew God but did not know Him as Father, we know Jesus as the tender Savior, but we do not know the full glory of who He is.

I believe John's encounter in Revelation 1 reveals the Father's intention to reveal the beauty of Jesus in a way we cannot anticipate. The Father is going to use the end times to set a stage for the glory of Jesus to be revealed in the sight of the nations. The church and the nations will be shocked and stunned by the beauty of Jesus that will be revealed at the end of the age. Therefore, we study the return of Jesus because it gives us a glimpse of what is coming when the Father reveals more of the beauty of Jesus. We want to feel what the Father feels about His Son and participate in the Father's plan to glorify His Son.[6]

There are aspects of Jesus' majesty only seen in His second coming. The apostles studied this subject and proclaimed it. We should do the same. We need to avoid unbiblical conclusions and unbiblical responses to the return of Jesus, but in doing so, we should not neglect this subject. It is vital for the church and deeply important to the Father.

Not only does the Father have deep desire for Jesus, Jesus also has deep desire for His people. Jesus prayed,

Father, I desire that they also, whom You have given Me, be with Me where I am, so that they may see My glory which You have given Me, for You loved Me before the foundation of the world. (John 17:24 NASB)[7]

---

[6] See Psalm 2:7–9; 110:1–2; Isaiah 9:6–7; 11:10; 42:1; Daniel 7:13–14; Matthew 3:17; 17:5; Luke 9:35; John 5:22–23, 27, 37; Ephesians 1:9–10; 20–23; Philippians 2:9–11; Hebrews 1:1–6; 2 Peter 1:17; Revelation 5:6–9.

[7] See also John 17:11, 21–23.

Jesus wants us with Him where He is, and He wants us to see His glory. This is not merely His heavenly glory; it is the glory that will be revealed when He returns as a Man to resurrect His people and restore creation.

We Love the Bible

The second reason we study the return of Jesus is because we love the Bible. There is a tremendous amount of information in the Bible about the end of the age. By a conservative estimate, there are over 150 chapters in the Bible where the primary subject is the time of Jesus' return.[8] By comparison, there are 89 chapters in the Gospels, so this is a significant amount of information. We do not want to avoid over 150 chapters of the Bible.

We may not understand the full meaning of every detail, but the fact that God gave these passages to us means He intends for us to grasp the main themes in them. Therefore, we should study them regularly and extensively just as we would any other part of Scripture. The key to grasping the meaning of these main themes is to discover how they relate to the story of redemption, and this is the approach we will take in this book.

We need to recover a biblical view of the return of Jesus. This is Jesus' story, and there is quite a bit of it in the Bible. Because we love Jesus and want to partner with the Father's plan to glorify His Son, we must understand these passages and respond to them in a biblical way.

John gives us a key for the study of Jesus' return:

For the testimony of Jesus is the spirit of prophecy. (Revelation 19:10)

The goal of prophecy in the Bible is to give us a testimony, or a witness, of Jesus. The study of the end times must be Jesus-centered, and when it is, it will cause us to love Him more.

---

[8] An example of a list of 150 end-time chapters can be found at www.mikebickle.org/resources/resource/2888.

JESUS' RETURN IS PART OF THE GOSPEL

The return of Jesus is part of the gospel message. If we only speak of the first coming without the second coming, our gospel message is incomplete. This does not mean that, every time the gospel is preached, we must talk about the return of Jesus, nor does it mean that speaking only of Jesus' first coming is ineffective. However, the first coming without the second coming is not the full gospel.

To understand the gospel, we have to view the cross correctly. The cross is an event with no equal. It is perhaps the ultimate revelation to humanity of who God is. It was the result of centuries of prophecy and fulfilled key promises God had made. The cross is often thought of as the climax of the redemptive story when, in reality, it sets the stage for the climax of history. *The cross does not fulfill all the promises of God; it secures them.* Jesus' return brings the fulfillment of promises secured at the cross—promises that include the resurrection from the dead, the judgment of the wicked, and the restoration of creation.

Because the first coming did not fulfill all the promises of God, the gospel is not just what Jesus has done; it is also what Jesus will do.

Paul said we are "of all men most to be pitied" if the future promises of the gospel are not true.

> *If we have hoped in Christ in this life only, we are of all men most to be pitied. (1 Corinthians 15:19 NASB)*

Paul also said all of creation is groaning for God to fulfill His promises:

> *For the creation waits with eager longing for the revealing of the sons of God. . . . For we know that the whole creation has been groaning together in the pains of childbirth until now. And not only the creation, but we ourselves, who have the firstfruits of the Spirit, groan inwardly as we wait*

eagerly for adoption as sons, the redemption of our bodies. (Romans 8:19, 22–23)

Accordingly, Paul said the gift of the Holy Spirit we currently enjoy is just a down payment of the future fulfillment of the promises of God:

In him you also, when you heard the word of truth, the gospel of your salvation, and believed in him, were sealed with the promised Holy Spirit, who is the guarantee of our inheritance until we acquire possession of it, to the praise of his glory. (Ephesians 1:13–14)

Paul knew the cross had secured God's promises, but without the second coming we do not receive our promised inheritance. *The New Testament gospel is a forward-looking message that sets our hope on the return of Jesus and everything that surrounds and accompanies that return.* Accordingly, the apostles had an apocalyptic view of history. They understood the return of Jesus was the only thing that could bring resolution to the crisis in the earth.

The apostles commanded the nations to repent because Jesus would return:

"And they [the apostles] are all acting against the decrees of Caesar, saying that there is another king, Jesus." (Acts 17:7)

"The times of ignorance God overlooked, but now he commands all people everywhere to repent, because he has fixed a day on which he will judge the world in righteousness by a man whom he has appointed; and of this he has given assurance to all by raising him from the dead." (vv. 30–31)

For the grace of God has appeared, bringing salvation for all people, training us to renounce ungodliness and worldly passions, and to live self-controlled, upright, and godly lives in the present age, waiting for our blessed hope, the appearing of the glory of our great God and Savior Jesus Christ. (Titus 2:11–13)

Things will not always be the way they are right now. Jesus is going to deliver His people. He will also judge the nations. He will rule as King. To unbelievers, the message of Jesus as sacrificial Savior is foolish,[1] but perhaps the most controversial part of the gospel is that the suffering Savior is also a victorious King who will return and dismantle the wicked powers, both human and demonic, that have influence in this age. The apostles' message of a King greater than Caesar fueled the early persecution of the church perhaps even more than the message of Jesus as a Savior.

The return of Jesus was the greatest hope of the New Testament church[2] and her motivation towards holy living.[3] The New Testament apostles preached an apocalyptic gospel as an example for the church in succeeding generations. We must follow their witness and set our hope where the New Testament church set it.

Well-known pastor and theologian John Piper summarizes the hope of the gospel this way:

> *Biblical hope is not finger-crossing. It is a confident expectation of good things to come. . . . We set our hope on the second coming of our Lord. . . . The second coming of Christ is the completion of his saving work. If you take it away, the whole fabric of his saving work unravels.*[4]

With this in mind, let's consider a few more reasons why we should study the return of Jesus.

We Want the Knowledge of God

Throughout the Bible, God has chosen to reveal Himself primarily by what He does. The Bible declares God's attributes, but most of the Bible does not consist of statements of His attributes; instead, it tells the story of His interactions with mankind. In those interactions, we learn who God is and what He is like. *The study of the return of Jesus is not primarily the study of end-time events. It is the study of a Person, and the beauty*

---

[1] See 1 Corinthians 1:18.

[2] See Acts 1:11; Acts 28:20; Romans 8:18–25; 1 Corinthians 15:19; Galatians 5:5; 1 Thessalonians 2:19; Titus 2:13; Hebrews 10:37; 1 Peter 1:13; 2 Peter 3:4–14; 1 John 3:2–3.

[3] See 2 Peter 3:11–14, 1 Timothy 6:14–16; 2 Timothy 1:12.

[4] John Piper, "Our Hope: The Appearing of Jesus Christ," *Desiring God*, May 18, 1986. Accessed April 14, 2017. http://www.desiringgod.org/messages/our-hope-the-appearing-of-jesus-christ.

of this Person is revealed in a fresh way by studying His story and His commitment to His people.

For example, God describes Himself as merciful, but when we see His mercy extended in the Bible towards David after his sin of adultery or towards the thief on the cross, it helps us grasp the vast mercy of God. We can be told God is faithful and believe it. However, once we experience God's faithfulness when we are in a hopeless situation, we truly know what God's faithfulness means.

God is not only revealed in the stories of what He has done; He is also revealed by the predictions of what He will do. God has revealed ahead of time how He will act in the future, so we will know what He is like. For example, the Bible tells us God will release His judgments and bring justice to the nations at the end of the age. Most of the earth right now is longing for justice, and it is the study of the return of Jesus that reveals God's passion for justice.

Whether or not we are conscious of it, our perspective on the return of Jesus dramatically affects how we view God. This was illustrated vividly during the Chinese Revolution. Western missionaries in China had taught believers they would be raptured by God before tribulation came. However, when the revolution began, Chinese believers suddenly experienced severe suffering and persecution. This suffering created a crisis—not a crisis about end-time events but a crisis about the knowledge of God.

Missionaries had taught an end-time view that communicated God would remove His people before they faced hardship. Suddenly, God's people found themselves in the middle of suffering. The real challenge was not a misunderstanding of end-time events. The real challenge was that they had believed in a God who did not want His people to go through suffering, and yet they discovered God does allow His people to pass through suffering. Their view of God was shaken because of their expectations about the end times. Not every part of what we believe about the end times has this dramatic an effect on our faith, but what we believe about the return of Jesus does profoundly affect the way we understand God.

When Jesus came the first time, He came in a way that was very different from what everyone expected. Though the Pharisees knew the Bible very well, Jesus was unlike what they had anticipated. The vast difference between who Jesus was and what they expected ultimately led to offense with Him and an inability to receive Him. In the same way, when Jesus returns, the revelation of who He is will create controversy and an opportunity for offense because of our assumptions about Him. Therefore, we must study what the Bible says about Him and His return to grow in our knowledge of Jesus.

It Is Our Hope

In any good story, the great climax comes near the end. The story of redemption is the same, and we need to recover a sense of anticipation, expectation, and awe at the way the story of redemption ends.

Many of us cannot conceive of God doing something on the scale of the flood or the Exodus in our generation, but the Bible teaches all these events in the past were prototypes of the end of the age. The flood was not the climax of history. The Exodus was not the climax of history. Something far greater is coming. It is hard to even conceive of the events of the Exodus happening in our modern nations, but the prophet Jeremiah predicts what is coming with Jesus' return is so dramatic we will forget about the Exodus:

> *"Therefore, behold, the days are coming, declares the Lord, when it shall no longer be said, 'As the Lord lives who brought up the people of Israel out of the land of Egypt.'" (Jeremiah 16:14)*

> *"Therefore, behold, the days are coming, declares the Lord, when they shall no longer say, 'As the Lord lives who brought up the people of Israel out of the land of Egypt.'" (23:7)*

The story of this age, like all good stories, reaches its climax as it approaches the end. Understanding this climax gives us tremendous hope for the future. No matter what happens between now and then, the end of the age will be an extraordinary event. What will follow it in the age to come is so great and glorious that we cannot even conceive of it:[5]

> *But, as it is written, "What no eye has seen, nor ear heard, nor the heart of man imagined, what God has prepared for those who love him"—these things God has revealed to us through the Spirit. For the Spirit searches everything, even the depths of God. (1 Corinthians 2:9–10)*

---

[5] See also Isaiah 65:17; 66:22; 1 Corinthians 15:24; 2 Peter 3:13; Revelation 21:1–4.

The Bible uses wedding-type language to describe the return of Jesus. For example, Paul compares his labor in the church to the preparation of a bride for Jesus:

> For I am jealous for you with a godly jealousy; for I betrothed you to one husband, so that to Christ I might present you as a pure virgin. (2 Corinthians 11:2 NASB)

In the book of Revelation, John describes the return of Jesus and what follows as a wedding celebration:

> "Let us rejoice and exult and give him the glory, for the marriage of the Lamb has come, and his Bride has made herself ready. . . ." And the angel said to me, "Write this: Blessed are those who are invited to the marriage supper of the Lamb." And he said to me, "These are the true words of God." (Revelation 19:7, 9)

The analogy of a wedding is one of the best analogies for how we should approach the subject of Jesus' return, because there is a big difference between the way a married woman and an engaged woman think about their weddings. For a married woman, her wedding is primarily a memory—an event that changed her life forever, but it does not dominate her daily emotions or her daily activity.

An engaged woman is completely different. She also does the necessary things of daily life, but she is focused on her wedding day. If you speak to an engaged woman about life, she quickly shifts the conversation to her wedding because she is fixed on that day and that event. It dominates her thinking, drives her decisions, and stirs her emotions. In a sense, her life revolves around her engagement and her wedding.

To use the wedding analogy, biblically, the cross is not the wedding; it is the engagement. The cross was the moment Jesus secured all God's promises. However, the fulfillment of all God has promised has not come. Like an engaged woman, we are called to be eagerly waiting with intense desire for the day when Jesus returns to fulfill all that the Father has promised.

Biblically, we are called to live like an engaged woman anticipating her wedding day, but too many believers live like a married woman remembering. We tend to think of the day we were saved as the great event in our lives, but that is simply not true. The day we were saved is the day God began His work to prepare us for the great day coming.

A Christian who is not interested in the return of Jesus is like a bride not interested in her wedding day; it is abnormal. Sadly, many in the church do not think often about Jesus' return because the subject has been neglected or taught in an unbiblical or unbalanced way. However, when it is taught in a biblical way, it should create a deep longing in our hearts and provoke us to engage God's mission to prepare the earth for the return of His Son.

We Want to Obey Jesus

In Matthew 24 through 25, Jesus gave His longest sermon on the end times. After describing end-time events, He compared His return to Noah's flood and gave several parables that indicated how we should respond to His return. In His teaching, Jesus made three main points:

- There will be a long delay before the end times. He will not come as quickly as many think. We should be faithful in that delay.

- When the end times come, they will come suddenly. We should recognize the season of time we live in,[6] but we must avoid trying to set a precise date for His return.[7]

- When the end times begin, there will be no time to prepare for them. We must live in such a way that we are prepared for the return of Jesus at all times.

The only way to respond properly to Jesus' teaching is to prepare the church in every generation for the return of the Lord. To be obedient to Jesus, this must be part of our discipleship. It is part of what Jesus commanded and, therefore, part of the Great Commission.[8]

The Father is giving His Son a "bride" out of the nations. Like any good father, He wants His Son to have the best possible bride. He will present Jesus with a people who are mature, glorious, and in full agreement with His Son. *In the same way that preparation for a wedding pre-*

---

[6] See Matthew 24:32–33.

[7] See Matthew 24:36–37.

[8] See Matthew 28:20.

pares a bride for her groom, studying the return of Jesus prepares the church to be joined with Jesus.

Not only does God want to form us into a companion for His Son, He wants us to be intimately involved in His plan to exalt His Son. Therefore, the study of the end times has missiological implications. It gives us God's objectives for the church and reveals His plan to partner with the church to prepare the nations for Jesus' return.

The New Testament instructs us to have an understanding of the end times and to be prepared for it. This does not mean we will comprehend every specific detail, but we should know the main themes of what is to come. Many people are familiar with Jesus' warning in Matthew 24:36 that we will not know the day or the hour of His return, but we must balance this with His statement in verses 32–33— that we should be aware of the times and seasons, and not be surprised by His return:

> *From the fig tree learn its lesson: as soon as its branch becomes tender and puts out its leaves, you know that summer is near. So also, when you see all these things, you know that he is near, at the very gates.*

Jesus also taught His return would be like the days of Noah:

> *For as were the days of Noah, so will be the coming of the Son of Man. For as in those days before the flood they were eating and drinking, marrying and giving in marriage, until the day when Noah entered the ark, and they were unaware until the flood came and swept them all away, so will be the coming of the Son of Man. (Matthew 24:37–39)*

In Noah's day, the judgment caught the earth by surprise, and they were unprepared. However, Noah was prepared for it. In the same way, the church should be prepared for Jesus' return. As Jesus said,

> *For this reason you also must be ready; for the Son of Man is coming at an hour when you do not think He will. (Matthew 24:44 NASB)*

Jesus spoke a parable about five wise and five foolish virgins. Both were waiting for a wedding that was very delayed. However, the wise were prepared for the coming of the bridegroom, and though they fell asleep waiting for him, they were ready for him when he arrived:

"Then the kingdom of heaven will be like ten virgins who took their lamps and went to meet the bridegroom. Five of them were foolish, and five were wise. For when the foolish took their lamps, they took no oil with them, but the wise took flasks of oil with their lamps. . . . But at midnight there was a cry, 'Here is the bridegroom! Come out to meet him.' Then all those virgins rose and trimmed their lamps. And the foolish said to the wise, 'Give us some of your oil, for our lamps are going out.' But the wise answered, saying, 'Since there will not be enough for us and for you, go rather to the dealers and buy for yourselves.'" (Matthew 25:1–4, 6–9)

To be obedient to Jesus' teaching, we must prepare the church for His return whether or not His return comes in our time. The apostle Paul taught the exact same thing:

While people are saying, "There is peace and security," then sudden destruction will come upon them as labor pains come upon a pregnant woman, and they will not escape. But you are not in darkness, brothers, for that day to surprise you like a thief. For you are all children of light, children of the day. We are not of the night or of the darkness. So then let us not sleep, as others do, but let us keep awake and be sober. For those who sleep, sleep at night, and those who get drunk, are drunk at night. But since we belong to the day, let us be sober, having put on the breastplate of faith and love, and for a helmet the hope of salvation. (1 Thessalonians 5:3–8)

The return of Jesus will come suddenly to the world, just as an un-expected thief comes in the night. However, the church will not be caught off guard the way the world will be. The church will understand the times and will be prepared for His return. It is important we avoid unbiblical preparation and date-setting, but we must also be obedient to Scripture and prepare ourselves and the church for Jesus' return and the unique dynamics that will accompany it.

We Want the Work of the Holy Spirit

The night before He died on the cross, Jesus spoke to His disciples about what would happen when He was no longer with them. It was an emotional conversation, and John recorded the details for us in his gospel. In this conversation, Jesus promised the gift of the Holy Spirit for the sake of the church:

> *I still have many things to say to you, but you cannot bear them now. When the Spirit of truth comes, he will guide you into all the truth, for he will not speak on his own authority, but whatever he hears he will speak, and he will declare to you the things that are to come. He will glorify me, for he will take what is mine and declare it to you. All that the Father has is mine; therefore I said that he will take what is mine and declare it to you. (vv. 12–15)*

Jesus told the disciples there were many things He wanted to share with them that they could not bear. Because of that, He was going to give them the Holy Spirit. Notice carefully what Jesus said the Holy Spirit would do:

- He would speak whatever He heard.

- He would declare the things that were to come.

- He would glorify Jesus by revealing to the church the things that belong to Jesus. (Note Jesus repeated this promise twice.)

According to Jesus, one of the reasons the Holy Spirit has been given is to instruct and teach us, from the Scripture, about the things that will come. When Jesus told us the Holy Spirit would declare to us the things that belong to Him, this includes His second coming and the aspects of His glory that are only seen in His second coming.

When we think of the ministry of the Holy Spirit, we tend to think about miracles, healing, and other gifts and works of the Spirit. These are all powerful and all important for the building of the church. However, when Jesus was facing the cross, He promised the disciples the Holy Spirit would come and give revelation from the Scripture of His return and His glory. Jesus knew that information would be critical for the church, so He gave us the Holy Spirit, and the Spirit is eager to give that revelation to us.

We should not neglect any aspect of the Holy Spirit's work. We need power for preaching. We need power to heal the sick. We need miracles and all the gifts of the Spirit functioning. We need the Spirit to release conviction on human hearts at the preaching of the gospel. And, according to Jesus, we also need the Spirit to reveal through the

Word of God what the Father has to say about the second coming of His Son.

We Want to Engage in Missions

In 1974, missiologist Ralph Winter shocked the missions' world with a new concept.[9] At the time, there was a witness of the gospel in each nation in the earth, and many were asking if this was the fulfillment of Jesus' command to spread the gospel to the nations. Ralph Winter and others searched the Scriptures carefully and discovered Jesus' command was not focused on political nations. Instead, it was focused on what we now call *people groups*, units of people with a common language and culture. Ralph Winter's research revolutionized world missions and shifted the focus from political nations to people groups.

Ralph Winter gained this insight by studying the return of Jesus and then applying it to the mission of the church. When we study the return of Jesus, there is a lot of information we find that helps us understand God's purpose for the church. *As we study what the Bible says about the end times, we want to approach our study in a missional way.* We want to let that information help us understand how to better cooperate with God's plan.

We are used to thinking of our mission primarily in terms of individuals responding to the gospel, but missions is much more. Biblically, it is laboring with God to prepare the nations for the return of Jesus.[10]

---

[9] Steve Shadrach, "The Legacy of Lausanne 1974: Forty Years Later and a Personal Look at the Man Behind the Revolution," *Center for Mission Mobilization*, September 15, 2014. Accessed January 22, 2018. http://www.mobilization.org/blog/the-legacy-of-lausanne-1974.

[10] See Matthew 28:20.

Part 2: Promises That Must Be Fulfilled—God's Promises to Israel and the Nations

THE PROMISES THAT MUST BE FULFILLED

The key to understanding history and God's activity in the earth is understanding two important parts of the redemptive story: God's promises and His covenants. God's promises are the specific commitments God has made. The redemptive story is designed to fulfill these promises. Covenants are agreements God has made with His people that include terms, conditions, and promises. Biblical covenants describe how God relates to His people and determine how His promises are fulfilled and how the redemptive story will conclude.

We will begin by examining specific promises God has made. These promises have the following key characteristics:

- They are made by God and secured by Him. Human sin does not eliminate the promises.[1]

- These promises have not yet been fulfilled, but they must be for the age to end. God's honor is at stake in the fulfillment of these promises.

- Jesus secured these promises, but He has not yet fulfilled them.

- These promises will be fulfilled at the same time and will be deeply interconnected.

- These promises will be fulfilled in the end times and ultimately by the return of Jesus. Therefore, they are central themes of the end times.

---

[1] For this reason, these promises are sometimes called *unilateral promises*, meaning they only depend on the ability of one party. Others have referred to these as *unconditional promises* because God is bound to them regardless of man's performance.

We cannot understand how God brings this age to an end without knowing these promises. Because of the limited scope of this book, we will only deal briefly with each promise. For a fuller, more complete discussion on these promises, see the book, *One King: A Jesus-Centered Answer to the Question of Zion and the People of God.*[2]

These promises declare a specific, positive future for Israel and the nations that God has committed to bring to pass. Human sin causes crisis, turmoil, and delay in the fulfillment of these promises. It also causes individuals to lose their participation in the promises. However, because these promises are guaranteed by God, they are not jeopardized by human failure, weakness, and sin. God will perform everything He has spoken.

The mission of God through the church in the nations is designed by God to play a critical part in fulfilling His promises. *God is not going to bring these promises to pass in isolation.* He is going to complete them in partnership with His people, so we want to understand the promises to better partner with God. *These promises are ultimately realized by the return of Jesus, but the labor of the church throughout history sets the stage for their fulfillment.*

Setting the Stage for the Promises

Genesis 1 opens with the well-known phrase, "In the beginning," as it lays the foundation for the story of redemption. After briefly describing creation, Genesis 1 through 11 sets the stage for God's plan for world redemption. It tells us how sin and tragedy were introduced into the human experience and records God's commitment to redeem His creation.

In the early chapters of Genesis, we begin to see the full effects of humanity's sin as humanity's situation grows increasingly grim. Families are destroyed, sons are murdered, and wickedness escalates so rapidly that God releases a global flood to stop the growth of human wickedness. Even after the flood, the earth is still left in a crisis because sin continues to afflict the earth. Every leader, even Noah, ultimately is

---

[2] This section is a revised and summarized form of "The Basis of the Gospel—Abraham's Promise" from the book *One King—A Jesus-Centered Answer to the Question of Zion and the People of God.* It is used with permission from Forerunner Publishing.

found incapable of redeeming humanity. *From the beginning, it is apparent the earth needs a new leader, a new man, to redeem and restore the human race.*

While the flood was still a recent memory, men decide to set up a challenge to God's authority on the plains of Shinar. They began to construct a tower in search for access to spiritual power that would allow them to challenge the One who flooded the earth. In this pivotal moment, God stepped in and separated the people by confounding their speech. Thus began the story of the nations of the earth.

Genesis 11 reveals these men were trying to avoid being "scattered" across the earth:

> *They said, "Come, let us build for ourselves a city, and a tower whose top will reach into heaven, and let us make for ourselves a name, otherwise we will be scattered abroad over the face of the whole earth." (Genesis 11:4 NASB)*

God wanted men scattered across the earth because He wanted there to be nations. Men did not want to be scattered across the earth, so they decided to resist God. God responded to their resistance by confusing their speech and dispersing them in judgment. Though there is judgment, there is also the promise of redemption. Beginning in Genesis 3:15, God promised a "Seed" is coming who will redeem and restore the human race.

The nations who were scattered as a result of rebellion will become a beautiful part of God's plan. God's plan to redeem the nations began in Genesis 12 when He chose one man to become the father of a nation He would use for the redemption of the nations.

God's Covenant with Abraham

While there are things from the Old Testament that are passing away, the Bible never says the entire Old Testament is passing away. We need to know the covenantal context of the Old Testament so we can recognize what is temporary and what is permanent in it. *The promises made in the Old Testament continue to drive the redemptive story forward far more than most people realize.*

God began His redemption of the nations with a covenant made with Abraham. This covenant is the foundation of the gospel because its success is guaranteed by God and not by Abraham. While many believers believe the Old Testament is passing away, it is more accurate to say the Mosaic covenant is passing away. *Abraham's covenant has not passed away.* It is very different from the law of Moses. We will examine how the law of Moses affects the redemptive story and the role that it plays in the next section, but we must first establish the foundation of God's covenant with Abraham.

The Abrahamic covenant is the origin of Paul's conviction that the good news of the gospel is righteousness comes by faith.[3] In Genesis 15:6, Abraham believed God, and God "counted it to him as righteousness." In a sense, both Jews and saved Gentiles are descendants of Abraham because he was born a Gentile and yet also become the father of the Jewish people.[4] His life is a picture of how both Israel and the nations must come to salvation, therefore, the apostle Paul identifies Abraham's covenant as the basis for the gospel:

> *Now the promises were spoken to Abraham and to his seed. He does not say, "And to seeds," as referring to many, but rather to one, "And to your seed," that is, Christ. What I am saying is this: the Law, which came four hundred and thirty years later, does not invalidate a covenant previously ratified by God, so as to nullify the promise. For if the inheritance is based on law, it is no longer based on a promise; but God has granted it to Abraham by means of a promise. (Galatians 3:16–18 NASB)*

> *And if you belong to Christ, then you are Abraham's descendants, heirs according to promise. (v. 29 NASB)*

These promises undergird the story of redemption and create a great tension throughout the biblical narrative as the prophets predict their fulfillment and, at the same time, wonder how God will ever bring these promises to fruition. The New Testament authors marvel at how Jesus' death and resurrection becomes God's means of securing these promises. These promises play a key role in redemption and a key role in Jesus' return. Therefore, the first step to understanding the end times is to understand these promises and what the Bible says about God's commitment to them.

---

[3] See Romans 4:3.

[4] See Galatians 3:29.

In Genesis 12, God begins to give shape and definition to His redemptive plan by calling out Abraham and giving him very specific promises:

> *Go from your country and your kindred and your father's house to the land that I will show you. And I will make of you a great nation, and I will bless you and make your name great, so that you will be a blessing. I will bless those who bless you, and him who dishonors you I will curse, and in you all the families of the earth shall be blessed. (vv. 1–3)*

God made three very distinct promises to Abraham. Each of these promises are key components of God's redemptive plan and all three —the promise of land, the promise of descendants, and the promise to the nations—must come to pass. *The conflict over these promises will set the stage for the final conflict at the end of the age.*

The Promise of Land

First, God promised Abraham a specific land. In Genesis 12:1, He tells Abraham,

> *Go forth from your country, and from your relatives and from your father's house, to the land which I will show you. (NASB)*

The whole context of the promise is Abraham's being sent to a new land that he will possess. The land is presented to Abraham as a permanent inheritance, so Abraham's descendants must dwell perpetually in the land for this promise to be realized. The inheritance is promised specifically to Abraham,[5] whom we know never owned the land.

Herein lies the tension: If God's promises are true, then how is it that Abraham never saw their fulfillment? If Abraham's death is the end of God's promises to him, the promise of the land is forever unfulfilled because Abraham never inherited the land, neither did he live to see his descendants inherit it. *To understand God's redemptive plan, we have to understand that these ancient promises have not yet come to pass.*

The book of Hebrews describes this dilemma when it tells the story of the great men and women of faith. Their faith was great because

---

[5] See Genesis 15:8.

they remained faithful even when they did not receive what God had promised them:

> *All these died in faith, without receiving the promises, but having seen them and having welcomed them from a distance, and having confessed that they were strangers and exiles on the earth. (Hebrews 11:13 NASB)*

> *And all these, having gained approval through their faith, did not receive what was promised, because God had provided something better for us, so that apart from us they would not be made perfect. Therefore, since we have so great a cloud of witnesses surrounding us, let us also lay aside every encumbrance and the sin which so easily entangles us, and let us run with endurance the race that is set before us. (11:39–12:1 NASB)*

The redemptive story deeply connects God's people—even across the generations. God's promises to the patriarchs were unfulfilled in their lifetimes, but they will come to pass as we play our part in the redemptive plan. Just as their faithfulness and obedience set the stage for our blessing, so also our faithfulness and obedience will play a part in their inheritance. Desire to see the patriarchs receive their promises should provoke us to lay aside everything that hinders us and labor with the same commitment they had.

Abraham's unfulfilled promises also set the stage for the promise of the resurrection. Abraham did not receive his promises in his lifetime, and he cannot inherit his promises as a dead man. The only feasible explanation for this dilemma is that a time will come in the future when God will raise Abraham (and the rest of the patriarchs) from the dead so they can receive what God promised.

The Promise of Descendants

Second, God promised Abraham descendants:

> *And I will make of you a great nation, and I will bless you and make your name great, so that you will be a blessing. (Genesis 12:2)*

Abraham was told his descendants would become a great nation that would make his name great. This statement speaks to the quality of Abraham's descendants, not just the quantity. This promise cannot be accomplished simply by a great number of people coming from

Abraham. It is only fulfilled by a nation who comes from Abraham and makes his name great by becoming a blessing in the earth.

Righteousness is what makes a nation great.[6] Therefore, Abraham's descendants must become a righteous and a holy people to fulfill this promise. In biblical thinking, the unrighteous are cut off from the earth,[7] but Abraham was promised his descendants would become such a blessing in the earth that it would cause the nations to honor Abraham's name. This explains why the Old Testament repeatedly predicts a day when Israel is holy and righteous.

Genesis 15 confirms this great nation must come from Abraham's physical descendants.[8] Therefore, God's commitment to bless the nations through Abraham must include the redemption of Abraham's own family.

This promise has never been realized in history. To fulfill His promise to Abraham, God must resolve Israel's failure to bring great blessing to Abraham's name and make Abraham's descendants the righteous people who God promised him they would one day be. This is the foundation of Jesus' promise in the New Testament to save Israel.[9]

These first two promises set the stage for one of the central themes of the end times: the resolution of Israel's crisis and the fulfillment of Israel's calling.

The Promise of Being a Blessing to the Nations

Abraham also received a promise for the nations of the earth. God promised Abraham that all the nations of the earth would receive blessing through His plan to make a great nation from Abraham:

> *I will bless those who bless you, and him who dishonors you I will curse, and in you all the families of the earth shall be blessed." (Genesis 12:3)*

---

[6] See Proverbs 14:34.

[7] See Psalm 37.

[8] See Genesis 15:4.

[9] See Matthew 23:39; 24:30; Acts 1:6.

This promise is the foundation of the New Testament promise that God will save a remnant from every people group on the earth.[10] The first two promises are specific to Abraham's natural descendants, but God also promised from the beginning that His plan for Abraham would be for Israel to become a great blessing to all the nations.

This means the idea of gentile salvation is not a new idea originating in the New Testament, and Paul refers to Genesis 12:3 as the first preaching of the gospel to the Gentiles:

> *And the Scripture, foreseeing that God would justify the Gentiles by faith, preached the gospel beforehand to Abraham, saying, "In you shall all the nations be blessed." (Galatians 3:8)*

From the beginning, God's plan with Abraham was for the sake of the nations. As a result, the salvation of the Jewish people and the salvation of the nations are deeply intertwined. God will not fulfill one promise or the other; He must fulfill all three. The crisis that unfolds on the earth during the end times is about the fulfillment of these promises.

When you plan a major event, there may be months of planning, but as the event approaches, everything accelerates as the different components necessary to the big event all come together at the same time. God's redemptive plan will feel the same way. For centuries, the nations have been prepared for the fulfillment of these promises, but as we get closer to the time the promises come to pass, it will feel like everything is suddenly accelerating as God brings all three promises together.

The Warning of Controversy

God told Abraham He would "bless those who bless" Abraham and curse those who dishonor him (Genesis 12:3). "Dishonor" in the ESV is translated "curse" in the New American Standard Bible and "treats you lightly" in the New English Translation. God warned Abraham there would be great controversy over His redemptive plan. There will be individuals who agree with and bless God's plan by blessing Abraham, and there will be those individuals who curse or treat Abraham lightly because of how God chooses to fulfill the three promises.

---

[10] See Matthew 24:14; 28:19; Acts 1:6–8; Revelation 5:9; 7:9.

Though it will become easy to take offense at God's plan, God warns that agreeing with His plan by blessing Abraham is the way to receive the blessing that will flow to the nations of the earth. This caused Paul to warn the gentile believers in Rome to not be arrogant towards the Jewish people even though most of them were unsaved.[11]

There is no way Abraham could have anticipated just how controversial God's plan would become. As this age comes to an end, the crisis around how God has chosen to bring all three promises to pass will go far beyond what anyone has anticipated.

As the redemptive plan unfolds, each promise becomes dependent on the fulfillment of the other promises because God has designed each promise to contribute to the completion of the others. He will not bring about one promise and abandon the others. *The Jewish people cannot receive their inheritance unless the nations come into the blessing of salvation, but the nations cannot come into their full blessing without the Jewish people receiving salvation and a land inheritance.* These three promises are three strands of one cord that cannot be broken.[12]

The Foundation of the Gospel

Genesis 12 establishes the three core promises that drive God's redemptive plan: (1) Abraham will have descendants who will become a righteous nation, (2) those descendants will permanently inherit a land as a righteous people, and (3) the nations will come into great blessing and salvation through the process. *These three promises become the foundation of God's mission in the world and are reiterated throughout the biblical narrative.*

Paul told the Galatians Abraham received the essence of the gospel in Genesis 12:

> *And the Scripture, foreseeing that God would justify the Gentiles by faith, preached the gospel beforehand to Abraham, saying, "In you shall all the nations be blessed." (3:8)*

The covenant declaration of Genesis 12 was followed by the covenant ceremony of Genesis 15. Chapter 15 is significant because it

---

[11] See Romans 11:20, 23–27.

[12] See Ecclesiastes 4:12.

will become the basis of the gospel and of salvation by faith.[13] Paul interpreted Genesis 15 as an ongoing covenant:

> For what does the Scripture say? "Abraham believed God, and it was credited to him as righteousness." (Romans 4:3 NASB)

We are saved by faith because Abraham secured his promises by faith. *Our promise of salvation is secure only to the extent that Abraham's promises are secure.* Jesus' suffering, death, and resurrection did not replace God's agreement with Abraham; it secured it and made the fulfillment of the covenant possible.

God only enters into covenant a few times in the Bible, and the encounter between God and Abraham in Genesis 15 is one of the great covenantal encounters in Scripture. In this encounter, God committed to Abraham that He would keep His promises on the basis of His character and strength.

Abraham had expressed his pain to God and asked for assurance that the promises of Genesis 12 would be fulfilled literally. Abraham only addressed two of the promises—the promises of descendants and land—but the covenant encounter of Genesis 15 was a confirmation of what was spoken in Genesis 12, and all three promises were confirmed by this covenant act.

> But Abram said, "O Lord God, what will you give me, for I continue childless, and the heir of my house is Eliezer of Damascus?" And Abram said, "Behold, you have given me no offspring, and a member of my household will be my heir." (Genesis 15:2–3)
>
> And he said to him, "I am the Lord who brought you out from Ur of the Chaldeans to give you this land to possess." But he said, "O Lord God, how am I to know that I shall possess it?" (vv. 7–8)

Abraham was in pain because he could not see any way for the promises to come to pass. He could not have one son, much less many descendants, and he was wandering like a stranger in the land he was supposed to possess. In the conversation, God repeated and affirmed His promises from chapter 12:

---

[13] See Romans 4:3.

And behold, the word of the Lord came to him: "This man shall not be your heir; your very own son shall be your heir." And he brought him outside and said, "Look toward heaven, and number the stars, if you are able to number them." Then he said to him, "So shall your offspring be." (Genesis 15:4–5)

And he said to him, "I am the Lord who brought you out from Ur of the Chaldeans to give you this land to possess." (v. 7)

After verbally confirming His promise, God entered into covenant with Abraham in a covenant ceremony during which He fully committed to perform the promises:

He said to him, "Bring me a heifer three years old, a female goat three years old, a ram three years old, a turtledove, and a young pigeon." And he brought him all these, cut them in half, and laid each half over against the other. But he did not cut the birds in half. And when birds of prey came down on the carcasses, Abram drove them away. As the sun was going down, a deep sleep fell on Abram. And behold, dreadful and great darkness fell upon him. (Genesis 15:9–12)

When the sun had gone down and it was dark, behold, a smoking fire pot and a flaming torch passed between these pieces. On that day the Lord made a covenant with Abram, saying, "To your offspring I give this land, from the river of Egypt to the great river, the river Euphrates, the land of the Kenites, the Kenizzites, the Kadmonites, the Hittites, the Perizzites, the Rephaim, the Amorites, the Canaanites, the Girgashites and the Jebusites." (vv. 17–21)

There are several key components to this covenant ceremony. *First, the ceremony was based on an ancient method of making an agreement.* In this ancient ceremony, two individuals would walk between the divided carcasses of dead animals to make a verbal statement of their commitment. The commitment was that it should be done to them as it was done to the animals if they should break their agreement. God wanted to assure Abraham that this was a permanent agreement by using an ancient ceremony Abraham understood.

Second, God did not allow Abraham to contribute to the performance of the covenant. Though the covenant was made with Abraham, when it was time to make covenant, God put Abraham into a deep sleep, leaving him unable to contribute to the covenant ceremony. This happened because Abraham's righteousness[14] had to come from his faith alone. Faith, or confidence in God's Word, was the only thing that God allowed Abraham to contribute.

Third, two parties had to walk through the sacrifices to make the covenant, but instead of God and Abraham walking through together, God walked through. The covenant was only between Abraham and God, and yet Abraham saw two manifestations of God, a flaming torch and a smoking fire pot,[15] moving through the animals together.

Two parties had to walk through the animals to confirm the covenant, and Abraham saw God walk with God through the animals. *This means God made covenant with God to guarantee Abraham's promises.* Considering other Scripture, the two manifestations of God Abraham saw were the Father and Son walking through the sacrifices. This was more than a symbolic promise; it was also a prophetic act. Because of Abraham's sin, and the sin of his descendants, a day would come when the Son would be sacrificed like the animals to preserve the covenant.

In Genesis 15 the Father and the Son made a commitment to each other to fulfill the promises made to Abraham, and in the New Testament, we see the intimate partnership between the Father and the Son in the work of redemption.

God's commitment to the promises He made to Abraham in Genesis 12 was on full display in Genesis 15. The dramatic covenant ceremony emphasizes that Abraham's righteousness has no part to play in the fulfillment of the promises. God Himself will secure the promises with His own righteousness and at the cost of His own blood.

Paul learned the concept of righteousness by faith from this chapter. He understood God's commitment to His promises was based on His strength and not ours—the promises would be fulfilled according to righteousness that comes by faith.

The Invitation to Obedience

God's promises to Abraham were unconditional in the sense that God guaranteed them. However, God also required Abraham to re-

---

[14] Biblical righteousness includes the idea of being faithful to perform your promises.

[15] Some translations translate this as a *smoking oven.*

spond in obedience through circumcision. The covenant was guaranteed by God's ability, but God gave Abraham the invitation to respond in obedience.

Throughout Abraham's life, we see him respond to God in genuine obedience while demonstrating weakness as he comes up short in other areas. This demonstrates two key principles:

- *God secures our promises and loves us in our weakness.* For example, Abraham lied about his wife twice when he was afraid, but his shortcomings did not disqualify him.[16] God recognizes our weakness, and He covers it with His strength.

- *God values our response.* Our seemingly weak *yes* is powerful to Him. This explains why God required Abraham to respond to the covenant through obedience in circumcision. Though God guarantees the covenant, we must respond in obedience. If we come short, He covers our sin through the blood of Jesus, but if we reject and refuse Him, we can end up separated from the blessings of His covenant.

Abraham's promises are a lens through which we can look at the Old Testament, because these three promises undergird the plan of God and the predictions of the prophets. The Old Testament consistently predicts a day will come when all of Israel is righteous (we could say *saved*),[17] a righteous Israel inherits her land permanently in peace and safety,[18] and the Gentiles worship the God of Israel.[19]

The Apocalyptic Fulfillment of the Promises

Throughout the Old Testament, we see the deep longing of the people for these promises to come to pass. We can also read the impas-

---

[16] See Genesis 12:11–13; 20:2–3.

[17] See Deuteronomy 30:1–6; Isaiah 4:3; 45:17, 25; 54:13; 59:21; 60:4, 21; 61:8–9; 66:22; Jeremiah 31:34; 32:40; Ezekiel 20:40; 36:10; 39:22, 28–29; Joel 2:26; Zephaniah 3:9, 12–13.

[18] See Genesis 12:1–3, 7; 13:15; 17:7–8, 19; 26:3; 28:3–4; 35:9–15; Leviticus 26:42; Deuteronomy 32:43; 1 Chronicles 16:17–18; Psalm 105:10–11; Isaiah 32:17–18; 60:21; Jeremiah 24:6; 32:40–41; Ezekiel 11:17; 36:26–28; Amos 9:15.

[19] See Genesis 12:3; Deuteronomy 32:21; Psalm 22:27; Isaiah 24:14—16; 42:10–12; 49:6; 56:6–7; 60:1–3; 65:1; Jeremiah 16:19–21; Amos 9:11–12; Zechariah 2:11; 14:16; Malachi 1:11.

sioned oracles of the prophets who predict a day is coming when God will fulfill the great promises. One of the great tensions of the Old Testament is how God is going to accomplish what He has said considering the condition of Israel and the nations.

As the Bible unfolds, the prophets begin to describe the fulfillment of these promises in very apocalyptic terms. They repeatedly portray a time coming that is far beyond any other time in history, and the prophets have trouble finding words to adequately describe the magnitude of God's end-time activity.[20] This time will go so far beyond the events of the ancient Exodus that even the Exodus will barely be remembered.[21]

Abraham's promises are repeated, developed, and reaffirmed throughout the Old Testament. These promises are one of the major unifying elements that bind together all the books of the Old Testament. Once we understand these three promises and God's commitment to fulfill them literally, key themes in the Scripture and of the end times can begin to make sense.

[20] See Jeremiah 30:7; Daniel 12:1; Joel 2:2; Matthew 24:21.

[21] See Exodus 34:10; Deuteronomy 30:1–10; Isaiah 11:11–16; Jeremiah 3:16-17; 16:14—15; 23:7–8; 30:8–1; Joel 3; Zechariah 14.

How God Will Fulfill the Promises

God's interaction with Abraham introduces several biblical patterns. These patterns reveal how God will bring His promises to pass:

- God's plan is going to involve profound partnership with man. God's plan will require His supernatural power combined with man's effort and participation. Abraham and Sarah have to do their part to have a baby, but God will have to miraculously touch Sarah's womb.

- God will accomplish His plan through resurrection. To fulfill His promises, God has to raise Abraham from the dead. This promise of resurrection becomes a pattern for God's dealing with His people. It is such a significant pattern that Jesus passes through death and resurrection to enter His glory.

- The promises will be fulfilled simultaneously and not sequentially. God's activity over time will set the stage for the fulfillment of the promises, and the fulfillment will then come suddenly and apocalyptically.

- Israel will become a picture and a parable to the nations, illustrating God's dealings with man. Israel will become a picture of the gospel and will be one of the ways God will demonstrate His commitment to His promises.

- God will provide the resolution for humanity's crisis. He will raise up a Man who will accomplish redemption and fulfill God's promises.

- God will prepare the nations before the great conclusion of His plan. God's people in the nations will play a significant role in preparing the earth for the realization of His promises.

As these patterns unfold in the Bible, we begin to see how God will fulfill the promises He made to Abraham. At the center of God's plan to accomplish everything Abraham was promised, we find two things —a divine King who will fulfill the promises and a new covenant.

A Divine King

In 2 Samuel 7, God's plan for the fulfillment of Abraham's promises became more specific through God's unique covenant with David:

> *"Now therefore, thus you shall say to My servant David, 'Thus says the Lord of hosts, "I took you from the pasture, from following the sheep, to be ruler over My people Israel. I have been with you wherever you have gone and have cut off all your enemies from before you; and I will make you a great name, like the names of the great men who are on the earth."'" (vv. 8–9 NASB)*

> *"When your days are complete and you lie down with your fathers, I will raise up your descendant after you, who will come forth from you, and I will establish his kingdom. He shall build a house for My name, and I will establish the throne of his kingdom forever." (vv. 12–13 NASB)*

The covenant made with David is related to the covenant made with Abraham. Like the covenant made with Abraham, God did not give David conditions that would determine the outcome of the covenant. The success of the covenant depended entirely on God's ability to fulfill His promise. God told David that His covenant with him would stand "forever" and he would not face the rejection Saul experienced:

> *"But my steadfast love will not depart from him, as I took it from Saul, whom I put away from before you. And your house and your kingdom shall be made sure forever before me. Your throne shall be established forever." (2 Samuel 7:15–16)*

As part of the covenant, God also promised David He would bring the Jewish people into their full destiny as a people and that they would dwell in the land securely and peacefully. David and his son Solomon ruled during the golden years of ancient Israel, but during that time

God still promised a future time when He would plant them in the land without any enemies:[1]

> *"And I will appoint a place for my people Israel and will plant them, so that they may dwell in their own place and be disturbed no more. And violent men shall afflict them no more, as formerly." (2 Samuel 7:10)*

Second Samuel made the future fulfillment of Abraham's promises directly connected to the promised Son of David—a coming King. This is the Old Testament foundation of Galatians 3:16:

> *Now the promises were made to Abraham and to his offspring. It does not say, "And to offsprings," referring to many, but referring to one, "And to your offspring," who is Christ.*

The promises made to Abraham will be fulfilled by the Man whom God has chosen. *The Messiah and Abraham's promises are inseparable because the covenant made with David is a continuation of God's covenant with Abraham.* When God made covenant with David, He revealed He would accomplish His promises through the rule and reign of His King. Because this King will reign forever, the promises are secure.

As Paul wrote, the promises made to Abraham ultimately belong to a specific Man, a specific "offspring" (ESV) or "Seed" (NASB) of Abraham. That "Seed" is Jesus. The "Seed" is referenced in Genesis, 2 Samuel, and Galatians:

> *And I will put enmity between you and the woman, and between your seed and her seed; He shall bruise you on the head, and you shall bruise him on the heel." (Genesis 3:15 NASB)*

> *Then the Lord appeared to Abram and said, "To your offspring I will give this land." So he built there an altar to the Lord, who had appeared to him. (12:7)*

---

[1] The Old Testament prophets' emphasis on Jerusalem and the throne reveals their focus on David's covenant as the solution for Israel's crisis. See Psalm 132:11; 89:3–4; Isaiah 2:1–4; 9:6–7; 16:5; 24:23; 32:1–2; 33:22; 40:1–11; 52:7–15; 65:19; Jeremiah 23:5–6; 33:17–26; Ezekiel 37:24–28; 48:35; Daniel 7:27; Joel 3:17, 20–21; Amos 9:11-12; Micah 4:1–5; 5:2–5; Zephaniah 3:14–20; Zechariah 9:9; Zechariah 14:1–21.

"When your days are complete and you lie down with your fathers, I will raise up your descendant after you, who will come forth from you, and I will establish his kingdom." (2 Samuel 7:12 NASB)

Now the promises were made to Abraham and to his offspring. It does not say, "And to offsprings," referring to many, but referring to one, "And to your offspring," who is Christ. (Galatians 3:16)

The promises made to Abraham are secured and fulfilled through a single Seed—Jesus. Notice Paul revealed *how* the promises will be fulfilled; he did not *reinterpret* those promises. Paul specifically mentioned the "promises" in the plural because he continued to expect the distinct fulfillment of all three promises.

It is important that the book of Galatians does not seek to redefine the unique promises given to the Jewish people and the Gentiles. If Paul had wanted to change the expectation that the three promises made to Abraham would be literally fulfilled, he would have written a much longer letter that redefined these promises. Rather than redefine the promises, Paul simply declared that Jesus was the only way to experience the fulfillment of those promises and to receive the Spirit:

In order that in Christ Jesus the blessing of Abraham might come to the Gentiles, so that we would receive the promise of the Spirit through faith. (Galatians 3:14 NASB)

Because you are sons, God has sent forth the Spirit of His Son into our hearts, crying, "Abba! Father!" (4:6 NASB)

For we through the Spirit, by faith, are waiting for the hope of righteousness. (5:5 NASB)

Jesus alone can secure the destiny of Jews and Gentiles. He alone is the One in Abraham's lineage who is righteous and, therefore, can administrate God's promises. He alone can make Abraham's descendants into a righteous nation. He alone can make Abraham's name great. He alone can enable Abraham and his descendants to possess the land they were promised in peace and righteousness. He alone can bring great blessing to the Gentiles.

Neither our Jewish nor gentile heritage gives us an advantage in securing our promises. The Jews will not receive their portion of Abraham's promise differently than the way the Gentiles do. It is only our relationship to Jesus that secures our participation in God's promises, and like Abraham, that relationship is based on a righteousness that comes through faith.

Ultimately, Abraham's promises were made to King Jesus. Therefore, when we are in right relationship with Him, whether Jew or Gentile, we are positioned to enjoy those promises.

Paul emphasized this point in the book of Galatians by reminding the Galatians they had received the Holy Spirit through faith in Jesus.[2] The gift of the Spirit was a key part of the fulfillment of God's promises in the Old Testament.[3] Therefore, if Jesus has authority to pour out the Spirit, then He has authority to fulfill the promises.

As the biblical story continued, the prophets received a glimpse of the beauty of this coming King:

The Lord says to my Lord: "Sit at my right hand, until I make your enemies your footstool." The Lord sends forth from Zion your mighty scepter. Rule in the midst of your enemies! Your people will offer themselves freely on the day of your power, in holy garments; from the womb of the morning, the dew of your youth will be yours. The Lord has sworn and will not change his mind, "You are a priest forever after the order of Melchizedek." (Psalm 110:1–4)

In the year that King Uzziah died I saw the Lord sitting upon a throne, high and lifted up; and the train of his robe filled the temple. Above him stood the seraphim. Each had six wings: with two he covered his face, and with two he covered his feet, and with two he flew. And one called to another and said: "Holy, holy, holy is the Lord of hosts; the whole earth is full of his glory!" And the foundations of the thresholds shook at the voice of him who called, and the house was filled with smoke. And I said: "Woe is me! For I am lost; for I am a man of unclean lips, and I dwell in the midst of a people of unclean lips; for my eyes have seen the King, the Lord of hosts!" (Isaiah 6:1–5)

---

[2] See Acts 2:1–4; Galatians 3:2, 5–6.

[3] See Isaiah 44:3–4; 59:21; Ezekiel 36:27; 37:14; 39:29; Joel 2:28–29; Zechariah 12:10; Luke 11:13; Romans 8:9, 14–16; 1 Corinthians 3:16; Galatians 5:5, 22–23; Ephesians 1:13–14; 2 Thessalonians 2:13; Titus 3:3–6; 1 Peter 1:2, 22; 1 John 3:24.

For to us a child is born, to us a son is given; and the government shall be upon his shoulder, and his name shall be called Wonderful Counselor, Mighty God, Everlasting Father, Prince of Peace. Of the increase of his government and of peace there will be no end, on the throne of David and over his kingdom, to establish it and to uphold it with justice and with righteousness from this time forth and forevermore. The zeal of the Lord of hosts will do this. (Isaiah 9:6–7)

"I saw in the night visions, and behold, with the clouds of heaven there came one like a son of man, and he came to the Ancient of Days and was presented before him. And to him was given dominion and glory and a kingdom, that all peoples, nations, and languages should serve him; his dominion is an everlasting dominion, which shall not pass away, and his kingdom one that shall not be destroyed. (Daniel 7:13–14)

Though Israel's prophets were primarily focused on the salvation of Israel, they predicted the coming King would also save the nations:

In that day the root of Jesse, who shall stand as a signal for the peoples— of him shall the nations inquire, and his resting place shall be glorious. . . . He will raise a signal for the nations and will assemble the banished of Israel, and gather the dispersed of Judah from the four corners of the earth. (Isaiah 11:10, 12)

He says: "It is too light a thing that you should be my servant to raise up the tribes of Jacob and to bring back the preserved of Israel; I will make you as a light for the nations, that my salvation may reach to the end of the earth." (49:6)

God has given one Man dominion over Israel and the nations. He will fulfill all of Abraham's promises by His sacrifice (first coming) and by His judgments (second coming).[4] Both are required for Jesus to complete Abraham's promises.

A New Covenant

The Abrahamic covenant not only finds its fulfillment in a coming King, but also in a new covenant. *This new covenant does not replace the covenant made with Abraham; instead, it enables Abraham's covenant to be ful-*

---

[4] See Isaiah 53:1–11; 63:1–6.

filled. This new covenant also resolves the challenge of the Mosaic covenant, something we will look at more in the next section.

The great challenge of the Mosaic law is that its just requirements expose our sin, yet it is unable to deliver us from our predicament. The new covenant is God's answer to the crisis of our sinful condition and our inability to obey God's just law.

This new covenant will last forever, because it is secured by the King who will rule forever—the King prophesied in 2 Samuel 7. God's chosen King and this new covenant are His permanent solution to mankind's condition. *The new covenant is a corporate agreement between God and His people that resolves the Mosaic covenant and fulfills the promises made to Abraham.*

This new covenant is declared in both Jeremiah and Ezekiel:

> *"Behold, the days are coming, declares the Lord, when I will make a new covenant with the house of Israel and the house of Judah, not like the covenant that I made with their fathers on the day when I took them by the hand to bring them out of the land of Egypt, my covenant that they broke, though I was their husband, declares the Lord. For this is the covenant that I will make with the house of Israel after those days, declares the Lord: I will put my law within them, and I will write it on their hearts. And I will be their God, and they shall be my people. And no longer shall each one teach his neighbor and each his brother, saying, 'Know the Lord,' for they shall all know me, from the least of them to the greatest, declares the Lord. For I will forgive their iniquity, and I will remember their sin no more." (Jeremiah 31:31–34)*

> *"I will make with them an everlasting covenant, that I will not turn away from doing good to them. And I will put the fear of me in their hearts, that they may not turn from me. I will rejoice in doing them good, and I will plant them in this land in faithfulness, with all my heart and all my soul." (32:40–41)*

> *"Nevertheless, I will remember My covenant with you in the days of your youth, and I will establish an everlasting covenant with you . . . so that you may remember and be ashamed and never open your mouth anymore because of your humiliation, when I have forgiven you for all that you have done," the Lord God declares. (Ezekiel 16:60, 63 NASB)*

"Moreover, I will give you a new heart and put a new spirit within you; and I will remove the heart of stone from your flesh and give you a heart of flesh. I will put My Spirit within you and cause you to walk in My statutes, and you will be careful to observe My ordinances. You will live in the land that I gave to your forefathers; so you will be My people, and I will be your God." (vv. 36:26–28 NASB)

This new covenant is going to bring all of Israel to salvation. The nation will be saved so thoroughly each citizen will know God—they will not even need teachers.[5] When she comes into the new covenant, Israel will be saved forever and permanently dwell in the land as God's holy people. This is the fulfillment of God's promises to Abraham. If God is this committed to the first two promises He gave to Abraham, He is also committed to the third promise to the nations as well.

To emphasize His commitment to His promises, God compared His ability to fulfill Israel's promises to His ability to uphold creation. Twice in Jeremiah, He said the sun, moon, and stars would cease if the people of Israel disappear from the earth.[6] God made this statement when Israel was being destroyed by Babylon and the people were being carried off into exile. This means God intends to fulfill His promises even if Israel experiences slavery, exile, or occupation by foreign powers.

God has not always preserved Israel as a political nation, but He has committed to preserve Israel as a people forever. *Therefore, just as the Babylonian destruction of Jerusalem in 586 BC did not end God's promises to the Jewish people, the Roman destruction of Jerusalem in AD 70 did not end God's promises to Israel either.*

The book of Hebrews describes how the glory of the new covenant surpasses the glory of the Mosaic covenant. The author quoted Jeremiah's prophecy of the new covenant and did not reinterpret Jeremiah's prediction that the covenant would save Israel and Judah to emphasize the fact that God will fulfill the promises made to Israel through the new covenant.

The new covenant will do what the Mosaic covenant never could—secure God's promises to Abraham, to Israel, and finally to the nations.

---

[5] See Jeremiah 31:34.

[6] See Jeremiah 31:35–37; 33:19–22.

For if that first covenant had been faultless, there would have been no occasion to look for a second. For he finds fault with them when he says: "Behold, the days are coming, declares the Lord, when I will establish a new covenant with the house of Israel and with the house of Judah, not like the covenant that I made with their fathers on the day when I took them by the hand to bring them out of the land of Egypt. For they did not continue in my covenant, and so I showed no concern for them, declares the Lord. For this is the covenant that I will make with the house of Israel after those days, declares the Lord: I will put my laws into their minds, and write them on their hearts, and I will be their God, and they shall be my people. And they shall not teach, each one his neighbor and each one his brother, saying, 'Know the Lord,' for they shall all know me, from the least of them to the greatest." (Hebrews 8:7–11)

In the New Testament, we find the fuller expression of the new covenant. It is secured by the death and resurrection of Jesus. His blood enables us to have restored relationship with God through a covenant that is secured by God's faithfulness and righteousness rather than through our righteousness. While most believers recognize salvation is offered to the nations through the new covenant (i.e., the third promise made to Abraham), the new covenant secures all three promises. The new covenant will do more than anyone expected it to do—particularly regarding the salvation of the Gentiles—but it cannot do less than it was predicted to do. *It must save Israel.*

THE FUTURE FULFILLMENT OF THE PROMISES

To grasp the redemptive story, we must recognize that Abraham's promises were secured by Jesus' first coming but have not yet been fulfilled. Many people assume the promises were fulfilled in the first coming, but this is not the case. It is important we examine a few passages in the Old and New Testament to demonstrate that the Bible predicts a future fulfillment of Abraham's promises.

Old Testament Expectation

There are some Old Testament passages that, at first glance, seem to indicate Abraham's promises were in some measure fulfilled. A few passages in the book of Joshua are examples:[1]

> *So the Lord gave Israel all the land which He had sworn to give to their fathers, and they possessed it and lived in it. And the Lord gave them rest on every side, according to all that He had sworn to their fathers, and no one of all their enemies stood before them; the Lord gave all their enemies into their hand. Not one of the good promises which the Lord had made to the house of Israel failed; all came to pass. (21:43–45 NASB)*

> *"It shall come about that just as all the good words which the Lord your God spoke to you have come upon you, so the Lord will bring upon you all the threats, until He has destroyed you from off this good land which the Lord your God has given you." (23:15 NASB)*

Some believers assume Abraham's promises were fulfilled because Israel possessed a portion of the land for several centuries and achieved a measure of renown under David's and Solomon's kingdoms.

---

[1] Psalm 105 and Jeremiah 11:5 are two other examples.

In order to interpret these passages properly, we have to view them in the full context of Scripture, and in that context, there are a number of reasons why these verses do not indicate Abraham's promises have been fulfilled.

For example, Hebrews 11:39–40 plainly states the patriarchs did not receive what was promised, because God has a greater plan of fulfillment involving both the Old Testament saints and New Testament believers:

> *And all these, though commended through their faith, did not receive what was promised, since God had provided something better for us, that apart from us they should not be made perfect.*

Isaiah and Jeremiah prophesied long after Joshua conquered the land and long after the reign of Solomon, yet they foretold a dramatic, future deliverance of Israel.[2] Jeremiah predicted this coming event would be so dramatic that the original Exodus would pale in comparison:

> *"Therefore, behold, the days are coming, declares the Lord, when it shall no longer be said, 'As the Lord lives who brought up the people of Israel out of the land of Egypt,' but 'As the Lord lives who brought up the people of Israel out of the north country and out of all the countries where he had driven them.' For I will bring them back to their own land that I gave to their fathers." (Jeremiah 16:14–15)*

> *"Therefore, behold, the days are coming, declares the Lord, when they shall no longer say, 'As the Lord lives who brought up the people of Israel out of the land of Egypt,' but 'As the Lord lives who brought up and led the offspring of the house of Israel out of the north country and out of all the countries where he had driven them.' Then they shall dwell in their own land." (23:7–8)*

All the way to the end of the Old Testament, the prophets continued to focus on Israel's redemption and possession of the land, telling

---

[2] See Isaiah 11:11–12, 16; 12:2; 25:1; 43:16–17; 51:10–15; Jeremiah 16:14–15; 23:7–8.

of a day in the future when these promises would be fulfilled.[3] These predictions do not make sense if Abraham's promises had already come to pass. Ancient Israel's possession of the land was a result of the promises God made to Abraham, and the ancient Israelites experienced a measure of God's faithful commitment to His promises. This is why Old Testament authors connected the possession of the land to the promises.

However, when we consider the entire Old Testament, the fact that Israel had enjoyed a measure of the promise in the land was obviously not enough to fulfill the promises or else these prophets would not have predicted a future day of fulfillment.

It is significant that the prophets used the language of the Exodus to predict a future day of deliverance. The ancient Exodus was the key event that led to ancient Israel's possession of the land and her establishment as a nation. When the prophets tell us there will be an Exodus event in the future that will completely overshadow the ancient Exodus, it reveals the ancient Exodus and conquest of the land were not enough to fulfill God's promises to Israel.

New Testament Expectation

The real shock of the New Testament is not that Abraham's promises have been altered, but rather the way God is going to fulfill them through the suffering, death, resurrection, and second coming of His Son. The New Testament reveals that fulfillment will go far beyond what Abraham would have expected, and the process of fulfillment will be far different than anyone would have imagined, but the New Testament affirms the Old Testament expectation of a literal, future fulfillment of the promises. This becomes readily apparent if we consider a few New Testament passages in their context.

Matthew

Matthew 21 through 23 tells the story of Jesus' entrance into Jerusalem as King and His subsequent rejection by the religious leaders of the city just before His crucifixion. In His response to their rejection, Jesus made a staggering statement:

---

[3] See Isaiah 4:3; 32:17–18; 45:17, 25; 54:13; 59:21; 60:4, 21; 61:8–9, 66:22; Jeremiah 24:6; 31:34; 32:40–41; Ezekiel 11:17; 20:40; 36:10, 26–28; 39:25–28; Joel 2:26; Amos 9:15; Zephaniah 3:9, 12; 12:13.

For I say to you, from now on you will not see Me until you say, "Blessed is He who comes in the name of the Lord!" (Matthew 23:39 NASB)

We have to consider this statement in the context of the entire passage to grasp what Jesus meant. He was not saying they would not see Him again in any way because He would be publicly crucified a few days after this. Matthew put Jesus' statement in context to two key events in the passage. The first was Jesus' entrance into the city the way Zechariah prophesied the Messianic King would enter.[4] The second, was the rejection of Jesus as King by the Jewish leaders.

Jesus had entered the city as its King but had been rejected by the leaders of the city. Therefore, when Jesus told the rulers of the city they would not see Him again until they blessed Him as the One "who comes in the name of the Lord," He predicted He would not enter Jerusalem again as King until the Jewish leaders of Jerusalem welcomed Him as the King sent by God.

In this one verse, Jesus made His second coming and His rule from Jerusalem as King dependent on the salvation of Israel. Jesus refused to be King over the Jews until a time when they willingly love and welcome Him. The fact that He made this prediction in Jerusalem emphasized His commitment to the land and the city.

Jesus affirmed a future fulfillment of the promise made to Abraham regarding his descendants. They must be "saved," which will result in welcoming Jesus as their King. Furthermore, this must happen in Jerusalem, meaning they must be saved in the land. Their salvation in the land will set the stage for the permanent inheritance of the land. *Jesus is so committed to a literal fulfillment of Abraham's promises, He will not rule on the earth as King without fulfilling the first two promises made to Abraham.*

Jesus did not stop with the affirmation of the first two promises. When the disciples asked Jesus what it would take to fulfill what the prophets had prophesied,[5] Jesus also affirmed the third promise made to Abraham:

---

[4] See Zechariah 9:9; Matthew 21:1–11.

[5] See Matthew 24:3.

This gospel of the kingdom shall be preached in the whole world as a testimony to all the nations, and then the end will come. (Matthew 24:14 NASB)

Jesus made His return dependent on all three promises. Not only will He fulfill the first two promises, He is also committed to the third promise. All the families of the earth—we would say "people groups"—will be blessed by the gospel before the end will come.[6] *The New Testament promise that every tribe and tongue must hear the gospel was not a new idea. It was a continuation of the Old Testament promise given to Abraham.*

A few verses after affirming this promise, Jesus reiterated His commitment to the salvation of Israel:

And then the sign of the Son of Man will appear in the sky, and then all the tribes of the earth will mourn, and they will see the Son of Man coming on the clouds of the sky with power and great glory. (Matthew 24:30 NASB)[7]

Because of the reference to mourning, many assume this verse refers to the mourning of the nations at Jesus' return. However, this is not the point of this verse. Jesus was referring to a specific event predicted by Zechariah:

"And I will pour out on the house of David and the inhabitants of Jerusalem a spirit of grace and pleas for mercy, so that, when they look on me, on him whom they have pierced, they shall mourn for him, as one mourns for an only child, and weep bitterly over him, as one weeps over a firstborn. On that day the mourning in Jerusalem will be as great as the mourning for Hadad-rimmon in the plain of Megiddo. The land shall mourn, each family by itself: the family of the house of David by itself, and their wives by themselves; the family of the house of Nathan by itself, and their wives by themselves." (Zechariah 12:10–12)

---

[6] See also Matthew 28:19; Acts 1:8; Revelation 5:9; 7:9.

[7] The word *earth* in Matthew 24 is a flexible word that can be translated in English as *earth* (the entire world) or *land* (a specific portion of earth). The context determines the way the word should be understood. In this case, it is a quote of Zechariah 12 which refers to a specific portion of earth, namely Judah.

Zechariah described a dramatic moment in Israel's future. He predicted a day when Israel would see Jesus as the One who was pierced by them but also for them. This revelation will result in great mourning, but it will be the mourning of repentance. It is the great day when Israel sees Jesus again, recognizes Him as the One who loved her all along, and mourns over how she rejected and resisted Him.

Zechariah used imagery from the story of Joseph. Joseph saved Gentiles (Egypt) and Israel (Jacob's family). In the same way, Jesus will save the Gentiles and Israel. When Jesus returns, Israel will mourn as she is reunited to Him just as the sons of Jacob mourned when they were reunited with Joseph and realized what he had done for them.

Matthew 24 through 25 is Jesus' longest teaching on the end-times, and in it Jesus makes two key points:

1. Abraham's promises are intimately connected. Jesus is committed to all three promises.

2. The promises are fulfilled by Jesus' return in the context of the end times.

Thousands of years before He spoke the words in Matthew 24, Jesus walked through sacrifices that foreshadowed His own sacrifice and made a commitment to Abraham to fulfill every promise. Thousands of years ago, Jesus stood before an ancient man in the middle of the Middle East, and He committed His life—His own blood—to fulfill everything He had promised. Matthew 24 reveals He has not forgotten His oath.

The Promises in Acts

Jesus spoke about the kingdom for forty days before His ascension. At the conclusion of those forty days, Jesus was asked a summary question about His teaching:

So when they had come together, they asked him, "Lord, will you at this time restore the kingdom to Israel?" He said to them, "It is not for you to know times or seasons that the Father has fixed by his own authority. But you will receive power when the Holy Spirit has come upon you, and you will be my witnesses in Jerusalem and in all Judea and Samaria, and to the end of the earth." (Acts 1:6–8)

The question was very revealing—Jesus' teaching had left a Jewish audience with the expectation the kingdom would be restored to Israel. When Jesus answered, He did not dismiss their expectation of a restored future for Israel, nor did He correct them. Jesus frequently corrected the disciples when they misunderstood Him or made wrong assumptions,[8] but in this case He did not correct them, indicating they had understood His teaching correctly.

Jesus had taught for forty days, and if He had meant to redefine their expectation regarding what would happen to Israel, He would have done it during that time. Instead, He left a Jewish audience with the continued expectation He would fulfill His promise to Abraham and make His descendants into a great nation.

Some Christians throughout history have believed the kingdom of God takes on a radical new direction after Jesus' first coming—a direction that no longer includes any specific purpose for Israel. However, Jesus not only affirmed Israel's future, but He also taught a restored, future kingdom for Israel.

In His answer, Jesus gave two very important pieces of information. First, He addressed the timing of the apostles' expectation. The restored kingdom would not come to Israel immediately. There would be a period of time. Second, Jesus connected Israel's restoration with the mission to take the gospel to the Gentiles. As in Matthew 24, Jesus emphasized all three promises. In Acts 1, Jesus made it clear the promises are inseparable, and He will not fulfill one without the others.

The book of Acts also reveals the apostles were looking for a future fulfillment of the promises. In Acts 2, Peter referenced Israel's future salvation by quoting Joel 2:32—

"And it shall come to pass that everyone who calls upon the name of the Lord shall be saved." (v. 21)

And it shall come to pass that everyone who calls on the name of the Lord shall be saved. For in Mount Zion and in Jerusalem there shall be those who escape, as the Lord has said, and among the survivors shall be those whom the Lord calls. (Joel 2:32)

---

[8] See Mark 8:33; 10:42–43; Luke 9:41, 49–50, 54–55.

Joel 2:32 predicts the day Israel cries out for salvation. It is a reference to the day Zechariah described when all of Israel would come to salvation:

> *"And I will pour out on the house of David and the inhabitants of Jerusalem a spirit of grace and pleas for mercy, so that, when they look on me, on him whom they have pierced, they shall mourn for him, as one mourns for an only child, and weep bitterly over him, as one weeps over a firstborn." (Zechariah 12:10)*

Peter's point in Acts 2 was that the outpouring of the Holy Spirit would lead to the moment Joel and Zechariah prophesied when everyone in Israel would call on the name of the Lord.

In Acts 3, Peter again predicted the future restoration of Israel:

> *That times of refreshing may come from the presence of the Lord, and that he may send the Christ appointed for you, Jesus, whom heaven must receive until the time for restoring all the things about which God spoke by the mouth of his holy prophets long ago. (vv. 20–21)*

Peter did not see a fulfillment of Israel's promises in Jesus' first coming, His ascension, or the present time when He is in heaven. He predicted a future day, an appointed time, when Jesus would return to fulfill the promises. This time will be the time when the things the prophets predicted would come to pass.

Peter did not redefine what the prophets had spoken; he expected a future, literal fulfillment of their words. He used the word *restoration* just as Jesus had in Acts 1, and Luke recorded this so we would make the connection. Peter, like Jesus, is referring to the restoration of Israel. The word Peter used for restoration (ἀποκατάστασις) was a reference to the Old Testament promise of Israel's final restoration. Peter would not have used this word if the promises had already been fulfilled. He also would not have used the language of *restoration* if the promises were going to come to pass through a "new" Israel without any connection to the Israel of the past.

Near the end of his ministry, the apostle Paul told the Romans he was in chains for the "hope of Israel"[9]—a statement demonstrating he shared Peter's expectation of Israel's future salvation.

The Promises in Romans

In Romans 9, Paul described his anguish over Israel's condition because he understood her election was irrevocable and God must fulfill her promises.[10] *Paul would not have been in anguish over his people if their promises had been fulfilled.* Paul even described his gospel mission to the Gentiles as a key part of God's plan to bring about these promises (Romans 10–11).

In Romans 11, Paul summarized his expectation for God to fulfill the promises made to the Jews and the Gentiles, revealing that he saw his mission through the lens of the three promises. He predicted both the "fullness of the Gentiles" and that "Israel will be saved":

Lest you be wise in your own sight, I do not want you to be unaware of this mystery, brothers: a partial hardening has come upon Israel, until the fullness of the Gentiles has come in. And in this way all Israel will be saved, as it is written, "The Deliverer will come from Zion, he will banish ungodliness from Jacob"; "and this will be my covenant with them when I take away their sins." (vv. 25–27)

Paul also summarized his mission in Romans 15:

For I say that Christ has become a servant to the circumcision on behalf of the truth of God to confirm the promises given to the fathers, and for the Gentiles to glorify God for His mercy; as it is written, "Therefore I will give praise to You among the Gentiles, and I will sing to Your name." (vv. 8–9 NASB)

Paul's conclusions are clear. Jesus came to confirm and secure the promises given to Abraham and Jacob. The covenant was not a single promise, but multiple promises and Paul referenced the fulfillment of all three. Through Jesus, God is committed to what He promised to Abraham which includes both his physical descendants and the salva-

---

[9] See Acts 28:20.

[10] See Romans 9:1–3; 11:29.

tion of the Gentiles. Paul's overview of the gospel reveals again that the promises are deeply intertwined and connected.[11]

The New Testament is not unclear about when the promises are fulfilled or whether they are literal. The great enigma is how God will accomplish His marvelous plan where the fulfillment of each promise ends up becoming a means to the fulfillment of the other promises. God will use something intensely negative—Israel's rejection of Jesus—to bring about the promise He made to Abraham regarding the Gentiles. In return, the Gentiles are going play a key role in the promises made to Israel.

The Promises in Revelation

Like Jesus, Peter, and Paul, John also predicted the future fulfillment of the promises. In his introduction to the book of Revelation, John summarized what the return of Jesus would accomplish:

> *Behold, he is coming with the clouds, and every eye will see him, even those who pierced him, and all tribes of the earth will wail on account of him. Even so. Amen. (v. 7)*

As in Matthew 24:30, this is a quotation of the mourning prophesied in Zechariah 12—mourning unto repentance at the return of Jesus. This verse does not describe the mourning of wicked nations at Jesus' return, but rather the glorious moment when Israel will come to repentance and embrace Jesus. The fact that John emphasized this passage in his introduction tells us how central it was in John's expectation. He expected the return of Jesus to fulfill these promises.

John also recorded some of the most vivid predictions of the salvation of the Gentiles:

> *And they sang a new song, saying, "Worthy are You to take the book and to break its seals; for You were slain, and purchased for God with Your blood men from every tribe and tongue and people and nation." (5:9 NASB)*

> *After these things I looked, and behold, a great multitude which no one could count, from every nation and all tribes and peoples and tongues,*

---

[11] See Deuteronomy 32:21; Romans 10:19–21; Isaiah 65:1–2; Romans 11:1, 11–12, 15, 25–31.

standing before the throne and before the Lamb, clothed in white robes,
and palm branches were in their hands. (7:9 NASB)

Yet again, we see the fulfillment of all the promises is associated
with the return of Jesus. In addition, by some counts, the book of Revelation has over five hundred references and allusions to the Old Testament, indicating there is still a future fulfillment for many Old Testament passages.

The Influence of History on Interpretation

If the Old and New Testaments are this clear about the literal, future fulfillment of the promises, why are there interpretations of the
Bible that consider the promises to have been fulfilled or to have been
redefined by Jesus' first coming? There are a number of factors that
have led to these other interpretations, but one we must address is the
interpretation of the Bible based on assumptions rooted more in historical events than the biblical text.

A key example of this is the effect of the destruction of Jerusalem
in AD 70 on biblical interpretation. The fall of Jerusalem and the subsequent Diaspora resulted in the vast majority of Jewish people being
driven out of the land of Israel. When Nebuchadnezzar destroyed
Jerusalem in 586 BC, within seventy years a significant Jewish population returned and began rebuilding in Jerusalem. After the Roman destruction of Jerusalem, no such return happened. For centuries the
land, and the Jewish people, seemed completely forgotten. It even felt
as though God had abandoned the promises.

This event combined with the fact that most of the Jewish people
did not embrace Jesus as Messiah made the literal fulfillment of Abraham's promises seem impossible to many gentile theologians. As a result, many theologians assumed that AD 70 was God's final statement
on Israel, and they developed systems of interpretation that viewed
Abraham's promises in an allegorical way. Given that there was no significant Jewish return and no Jewish state for nearly two thousand
years, it seemed reasonable for theologians to try to find alternate ex-
planations for prophecies that seemed impossible.

What seemed impossible for centuries, suddenly became possible in
1948. The establishment of modern Israel and the subsequent return

to the land are a warning we should not dismiss what the Bible plainly says simply because it seems impossible.

In retrospect, to say God "fulfilled" or "transitioned" Israel's promises in the first century AD simply does not make sense. Israel's experience in the first century was disastrous. The nation was not saved. On the contrary, according to Paul, most were hardened.[12] Not only did Israel not truly possess the land due to being under Roman occupation, most of those in the land were driven out by the Romans. To say this is the fulfillment of the promise that brings Israel into her destiny violates all logic and common sense. Israel's situation in the first century was traumatic, and to make that the fulfillment of the promises violates the plain reading of God's promises.

The truth is our entire redemption is based on God doing the impossible. The Bible tells us God became a human being. He suffered, died, and rose from the dead. His death can provide atonement for all humanity. As a man He ascended to His throne in the heavens. He is going to return visibly in the sky as a man. None of this would have been anticipated by the prophets, and every bit of it is a human impossibility. However, it is all the gospel.

We must be willing to live in the tension of standing with what the Word of God plainly says even when the possibility of the literal fulfillment of it seems unfeasible to us. And we must beware of interpreting the Bible through our own historical lens or through the lens of what we think is reasonable.

---

[12] See Romans 11:7.

GOD MUST FULFILL HIS PROMISES

We have seen how God's promises drive the biblical narrative. We have also seen that God's promises remain unfulfilled and both the Old and New Testament authors expected a future fulfillment of the promises. Before we finish this section, there are two more points we need to make. The first is that God's honor is at stake in His ability to fulfill His promises. The second is that the controversy over these promises is growing in the nations.

God's Honor Is at Stake

God's honor is at stake in the literal fulfillment of His promises. This is illustrated by Moses' intercession for Israel in Deuteronomy 9:

> *And I prayed to the Lord, "O Lord God, do not destroy your people and your heritage, whom you have redeemed through your greatness, whom you have brought out of Egypt with a mighty hand. Remember your servants, Abraham, Isaac, and Jacob. Do not regard the stubbornness of this people, or their wickedness or their sin, lest the land from which you brought us say, 'Because the Lord was not able to bring them into the land that he promised them, and because he hated them, he has brought them out to put them to death in the wilderness.' For they are your people and your heritage, whom you brought out by your great power and by your outstretched arm." (vv. 26–29)*

At the time of Moses' intercession, Israel was deep in sin and provoked God to judgment according to the terms of the covenant. God had given Moses an offer to make Him into a great nation so He could judge Israel while keeping His promises.[1] Moses challenged God that

---

[1] See Exodus 32:10.

He must literally fulfill His promises or be humiliated before the nations.

Even when God's people are rebellious, God's honor is at stake in the fulfillment of His promises. God may bring His promises to pass in shocking and surprising ways, but Moses recognized He must accomplish His promises in a way that remains true to what He told Abraham.

Abraham's promises are a significant part of the "why" behind the "what" of end-time events because the end of the age is designed to be God's great climatic fulfillment of these promises. As a result, end-time passages typically emphasize the salvation of the Jewish people, the land of Israel (specifically, the city of Jerusalem), and the mention of the salvation of Gentiles.

The Growing Controversy over the Promises

When we look at the last hundred years of history through the lens of each promise, we see a growing escalation in the battle over the promises. We see clear signs of God's commitment to each promise as well as intensifying resistance to each one. The closer we get to the return of the Lord, the more extreme the conflict over these promises will become, setting the stage for the end times which will be the time of the most intense global conflict over these promises. God will release unparalleled power in the nations to accomplish His purposes, and the enemy will release unprecedented opposition.

Promise 1—The Land

The Bible tells us that Jewish possession of the land will become one of the main controversies in the earth,[2] and now for the first time in two thousand years, there is a Jewish state in the land setting the context for that controversy. We live in the first generation where the fulfillment of the land passages is suddenly possible.

Though the modern state of Israel is not a saved nation, the very presence of that state is a thunderous statement from God that He intends to fulfill the promise He made regarding the land. Historically, the conflict over the land of Israel was a regional conflict based on a struggle over trade routes or the ambition of provincial empires. The conflict over Israel has never been a global issue affecting the nations of the earth until now. Because Is-

---

[2] See Isaiah 34, 63; Joel 3; Zechariah 12–14; Revelation 11.

rael has existed as long as most of us have been alive, it's easy to miss how stunning and unprecedented all of this is.

The modern world no longer relies on the ancient trade routes that motivated Israel's ancient aggressors. Now, the nations oppose Israel for religious and ideological reasons, and the stage is being set in the nations for the final conflict over the land.

Promise 2—Israel's Salvation

The Bible tells us the salvation of the Jewish people will be contested—even to the point of attempted extermination—because the end of the age will result in their salvation.[3] We live in a time where there is a historical salvation occurring among the Jewish people. Though Israel is not yet saved, messianic believers are taking their place.

Across the church, there is also a growing awareness of the need to understand what the Bible says about the salvation of Israel. The Lord is demonstrating His commitment to this promise.

At the same time, the twentieth century saw the horror of the Holocaust—the most gruesome attempt yet at preventing the salvation of the Jewish people—and it did not end with the Holocaust. The modern state of Israel has provoked anti-Semitism in an unprecedented way, and there are calls in some parts of the Islamic world for her destruction. In some cases, there are accompanying calls for the annihilation of the Jewish people using anti-Semitic language that goes far beyond anything propagated by Adolf Hitler. This is also not limited to the Middle East. In May 2016, half of the French soldiers deployed in France were engaged in protecting synagogues and Jewish schools.[4]

The contest of Israel's salvation is rising in the nations.

Promise 3—The Nations

The Bible predicts a remnant in all the nations must worship Israel's God before the age will end,[5] and we are on the brink of an in-

---

[3] See Daniel 7:21; Jeremiah 31:31–40; Zechariah 12:10; Matthew 23:39; 24:30; Romans 11:25–26; Revelation 1:7; 12:17.

[4] Meotti, Giulio. "The Great Western Retreat." Gatestone Institute. http://www.gatestoneinstitute.org/7938/western-retreat (accessed February 5, 2018).

[5] See Matthew 24:14; Romans 10:19–21; Revelation 5:9; 7:9.

credible milestone in redemptive history: For the first time in history, it is now possible for the gospel to reach every tribe and tongue. Evangelism is accelerating and millions have come to the gospel in the last century. We live in a time when the fastest growing church in the world is in a nation hostile to the gospel,[6] and millions of people have gathered for mega crusades that would have been unimaginable in a previous generation.[7]

At the same time, more Christians have been martyred in the last century than in all previous centuries combined,[8] and persecution is on the rise in a number of nations that are hostile to the gospel. Though the number of unreached people groups has dropped dramatically, many of the remaining people groups will be the most difficult to reach.

---

[6] Howard, Mark. "The Story of Iran's Church in Two Sentences." The Gospel Coalition. https://www.thegospelcoalition.org/article/the-story-of-the-irans-church-in-two-sentences/ (accessed February 5, 2018).

[7] CBN News. "30 Million People Expected for Reinhard Bonnke's Farewell Mission in Africa." CBN.com. http://www1.cbn.com/cbnnews/world/2017/october/30-million-people-expected-for-reinhard-bonnkes-farewell-crusade-in-africa (accessed February 5, 2018).

[8] Johnson, Todd M. "Christian Martyrdom: A Global Demographic Assessment," Gordon Conwell. http://www.gordonconwell.edu/ockenga/research/documents/TheDemographicsofChristianMartyrdom.pdf (accessed February 5, 2018).

Part 3: What Must Be Resolved—The Crisis of the Covenant

Israel's Covenantal Dilemma

We have examined the promises God must fulfill and how they shape the end-time story. However, not only are there promises that must be fulfilled, there are also specific covenantal issues that must be finally resolved. These covenantal issues keep Israel and the nations—but particularly Israel—from experiencing the fullness of God's promises. We can call this *the crisis of the covenant*. This crisis is frequently overlooked, but we need to understand the role it plays in setting the stage for Jesus' return.

The covenantal crisis is the result of the terms of the Mosaic covenant. If we do not comprehend this crisis or the process by which it is resolved, it is difficult to fully grasp the end times. Much of the confusion about the end times is due to not understanding the role the Mosaic covenant plays.

Many Christians believe the Mosaic covenant no longer has any effect on Israel or the nations, but that is not true. Jesus has secured the new covenant and the resolution of the Mosaic covenant, but there is a process by which the victory of the cross resolves *every* issue related to the Mosaic covenant. This process will be completed during the end times and is a key part of the end-time drama.

Many people assume everything in the Old Testament has passed away. As we saw when we examined the promises of God, this is not true. Some things passed away as a result of the new covenant, some things are passing away, and some things remain. We need to know which things have passed away and which remain so we can properly interpret the New Testament.

The Mosaic Covenant and Jewish Identity

When we deal with the Mosaic covenant, it is important to know the difference between living under the Mosaic covenant and living a

Jewish expression of life that incorporates elements of Jewish life and identity. In the time of the New Testament, the great challenge was how Gentiles could be part of the people of God. As a result, the New Testament authors made it clear believers from the nations did not need to "convert" to a Jewish lifestyle or take on a Jewish identity. Sadly, as the years progressed, and the church became predominantly gentile, certain parts of the church demanded Jewish believers completely abandon their Jewish identity—an idea that would have been foreign to the New Testament church.

After two thousand years of a primarily gentile Christianity, our challenge is the opposite of what the first-century church faced. The question is no longer can the Gentiles come into the family of God, but instead it is this: How should the predominantly gentile church embrace and honor Jewish believers? In the same way the early church made room for gentile believers, the global church now needs to do the same for Jewish believers.

When we speak of the Mosaic covenant passing away, we are referring to the fact that the Mosaic covenant and its curses are no longer binding on those who are followers of Jesus. However, when we speak of freedom from the Mosaic covenant, that does not mean Jewish believers should abandon their Jewish identity.

The Mosaic covenant is a key part of Israel's story in the Old Testament, but it does not define every aspect of Israel. Many other aspects of Jewish life rooted in the Old Testament are not part of the Mosaic covenant and, therefore, should continue to be a part of Jewish life for followers of Jesus. It is beyond the scope of this book to deal with the issue in detail, but it is imperative that the church recognizes the validity of a Jewish expression of faith rooted in Israel's history.

The Impact of the Mosaic Covenant

Just as we need to understand how God's Old Testament promises continue to drive the redemptive story, we also need to understand the things in the Old Testament that have been superseded and how God plans to resolve them.

In this section, we will deal primarily with the Mosaic covenant, which refers to the covenant made between God and Israel at Sinai. Many believers assume that it is no longer relevant to God's redemptive plan because it has been superseded, but this is not true. We need to examine how it continues to affect Israel and the nations, and the specific role it plays in the end of the age.

Before we consider the Mosaic covenant's ongoing influence, we need to begin with a proper perspective of the covenant. *Many Christians think of the Mosaic covenant only in negative terms, but the same God who gave us the new covenant gave the Mosaic covenant to steward Israel until the new came.*

Some theologians have made the error of treating law and grace as though they were mutually exclusive,[1] but the same God who gave us the law also offers grace. The issue with the law is not the law itself but the wickedness of the human heart that rebels against the law of God:

> *So then, the Law is holy, and the commandment is holy and righteous and good. Therefore did that which is good become a cause of death for me? May it never be! Rather it was sin, in order that it might be shown to be sin by effecting my death through that which is good, so that through the commandment sin would become utterly sinful. (Romans 7:12–13 NASB)*

Modern Western thinking tends to rebel against any law or restraint as *legalism*, but this is not a biblical idea. The law of God is good, and it extends beyond the unique requirements of the Mosaic covenant.

Within the Mosaic covenant, we can see the mercy of God setting the stage for the new covenant. When sin occurred, there were instructions for the restoration of relationships. Some people only highlight the punishments of the Mosaic covenant, but God also provided a means for restoration. The entire sacrificial system was given as a picture of God's desire to restore fellowship. God was slow to enact the punishments of the Mosaic covenant and quick to offer mercy to those who repented.

The covenant gave us a picture of both the kindness and the severity of God. The covenant provided both a picture of God's discipline

---

[1] This ranges from the negative attitude most Christians have towards the law to more extreme examples such as Classical Dispensationalism. Classic Dispensationalism was a theological system that proposed there were two people of God—Israel and the church—with two different plans of salvation. Though it is no longer widespread, it had a significant impact on how people viewed Israel in the twentieth century.

and a picture of his mercy and redemption. Therefore, we must reject the unbiblical heresy that the God of the Old Testament is some sort of vengeful God who is different in His essential nature from the God of the New Testament.

Israel's Covenant Encounter

When God made covenant with Israel at Sinai, He came down visibly on a mountain and spoke audibly to an entire nation, inviting the nation's people to come into covenant with Him as a people.[2] The nation accepted the terms of the agreement and entered into covenant. *Israel's encounter with God at Sinai is the only time God visibly and audibly offered a contract, or covenant, to an entire nation with detailed terms for blessing and for cursing.*[3]

While some denigrate the Mosaic covenant, it is an event without parallel and deserves serious respect. Moses reminded Israel how significant the covenant encounter was:

> *"Did any people ever hear the voice of a god speaking out of the midst of the fire, as you have heard, and still live? Or has any god ever attempted to go and take a nation for himself from the midst of another nation, by trials, by signs, by wonders, and by war, by a mighty hand and an outstretched arm, and by great deeds of terror, all of which the Lord your God did for you in Egypt before your eyes?" (Deuteronomy 4:33–34)*

The covenant made at Sinai was not simply a legal agreement for God. It was a profoundly emotional event God described the way a man would describe his wedding day:[4]

> *"Then I passed by you and saw you, and behold, you were at the time for love. I also swore to you and entered into a covenant with you so that you became Mine," declares the Lord God. (Ezekiel 16:8 NASB)*

---

[2] See Exodus 19:1–20:21. The covenant is summarized in Deuteronomy 28–30.

[3] There are parallels between the encounter at Sinai in the ministry of Jesus and in Acts 2, but Israel's encounter with God at Sinai is unique in terms of the offer of a covenant with specific terms.

[4] See also Hosea 2:15.

This gives us insight into God's relationship with Israel. Even after Israel rebelled in the wilderness, God remembered the covenant encounter with deep emotion and affection:

"Go and proclaim in the ears of Jerusalem, saying, 'Thus says the Lord, "I remember concerning you the devotion of your youth, the love of your betrothals, your following after Me in the wilderness, through a land not sown."'" (Jeremiah 2:2 NASB)

From God's perspective, this covenant is part of an ongoing story—one that He is very passionate about. We cannot simply dismiss the Mosaic covenant as "Old Testament." We must recognize its full significance and how it relates to other covenants.

The Key Differences of the Mosaic Covenant

There are two key differences between the covenants God made with Abraham and David and the one He made with Israel at Sinai.

The first key difference is that God offered the nation an agreement with specific terms. The terms included blessings and curses that were dependent on Israel's behavior. God declared His permanent commitment to Israel in the covenant, but He offered specific terms to the nation, and the nation's obedience or rebellion would determine if she experienced blessing or cursing as a result of the covenant. *The outcome of the Mosaic covenant was dependent on both the obedience of the people to God's terms and on God's faithfulness.*

The new covenant and the covenants made with Abraham and David are very different because they are all declarations of what God will do. In these covenants, God did not make the outcome of the respective covenants contingent on the human response. Abraham or David could have responded in such a way that he did not enjoy the benefits of covenant, but God was bound to His word, and He personally guaranteed the outcome of these covenants.

Jeremiah specifically noted the difference between the new covenant and the covenant made at Sinai:

"Behold, days are coming," declares the Lord, "when I will make a new covenant with the house of Israel and with the house of Judah, not like the covenant which I made with their fathers in the day I took them by the hand to bring them out of the land of Egypt, My covenant which they

broke, although I was a husband to them," declares the Lord. (Jeremiah 31:31–32 NASB)

The second key difference in this covenant was that God made covenant at Sinai with a nation rather than an individual. Though it is referred to as the Mosaic covenant, God did not make the covenant with Moses. God offered the covenant to the nation of Israel and the entire nation audibly affirmed the terms of this covenant with God. The biblical description of this covenant event is stunning:[5]

So Moses came and called the elders of the people, and set before them all these words which the Lord had commanded him. All the people answered together and said, "All that the Lord has spoken we will do!" And Moses brought back the words of the people to the Lord. The Lord said to Moses, "Behold, I will come to you in a thick cloud, so that the people may hear when I speak with you and may also believe in you forever." Then Moses told the words of the people to the Lord. (Exodus 19:7–9 NASB)

So it came about on the third day, when it was morning, that there were thunder and lightning flashes and a thick cloud upon the mountain and a very loud trumpet sound, so that all the people who were in the camp trembled. And Moses brought the people out of the camp to meet God, and they stood at the foot of the mountain. Now Mount Sinai was all in smoke because the Lord descended upon it in fire; and its smoke ascended like the smoke of a furnace, and the whole mountain quaked violently. (vv. 16–18 NASB)

"Has any people heard the voice of God speaking from the midst of the fire, as you have heard it, and survived?" (Deuteronomy 4:33 NASB)

"The Lord our God made a covenant with us at Horeb. The Lord did not make this covenant with our fathers, but with us, with all those of us alive here today. The Lord spoke to you face to face at the mountain from the midst of the fire." (5:2–4 NASB)

This encounter between God and Israel bound the entire nation to the terms and conditions of the covenant. These terms are summa-

---

[5] See also Deuteronomy 4:9–13, 32–36; 5:1–4.

rized in Leviticus 26 and Deuteronomy 28 through 30. They set the context for Israel's relationship with God throughout the Old Testament.

For example, in Leviticus 26, Moses summarized the blessings for obedience, curses for disobedience, and God's ongoing commitment to Israel despite her disobedience:

> *"If you walk in my statutes and observe my commandments and do them, then I will give you your rains in their season, and the land shall yield its increase, and the trees of the field shall yield their fruit. Your threshing shall last to the time of the grape harvest, and the grape harvest shall last to the time for sowing. And you shall eat your bread to the full and dwell in your land securely."* (Leviticus 26:3–5)

> *"But if you will not listen to me and will not do all these commandments. . . . ."* (vv. 14, 17–19)

> *"Yet for all that, when they are in the land of their enemies, I will not spurn them, neither will I abhor them so as to destroy them utterly and break my covenant with them, for I am the Lord their God. But I will for their sake remember the covenant with their forefathers, whom I brought out of the land of Egypt in the sight of the nations, that I might be their God: I am the Lord."* (vv. 44–45)

God's message was simple: The outcome of the covenant was dependent on the nation. He would respond to her obedience with blessing and her disobedience with curses. However, God's final statement to Israel was that He would keep covenant with her despite her sin. God had not yet explained how He would do it, but He clearly indicated He would find a way to keep covenant when Israel broke the Mosaic covenant.

The Sin of a Minority Impacts the Majority

The curses of the law were a constant threat to Israel's promises because they made the possession of Israel's inheritance dependent upon Israel's ability to keep the law. This was illustrated in the sin of Achan during the conquest of Canaan.

When the Israelites conquered Jericho, God prohibited the Israelites from taking any treasure for personal gain. Achan ignored this command and took things he found in the siege on Jericho. As a result of his disobedience, the Israelites were defeated in the next battle, and Joshua had to deal with the sin so that the Lord's favor could return to Israel.[6]

What happened with Achan was a strong message to the nation: *Because the Mosaic covenant was made with the nation, the sin of a minority could put the entire nation in jeopardy.* Because the sin of a remnant could cause the entire nation to experience God's judgment, an impossible situation emerged.

God had promised Abraham a time would come when his descendants would be righteous and inherit a land permanently in peace and safety. However, the law given through Moses created a situation where the people could not dwell in the land safely unless all of the people perfectly kept the law, a situation that could never happen.

Israel agreed to the Mosaic covenant as a nation and bound all her descendants to the terms of the covenant. *Israel entered into the Mosaic covenant as a nation, and Israel must also come out of the covenant as a nation.* Until that happens, any sin in the nation leaves the entire nation vulnerable to the curses of the covenant.

In the course of time, Israel failed to live up to the demands of the covenant. Israel did not fail because the terms of the covenant were too demanding or because she was more wicked than other nations. Israel failed simply because she was human, and human strength alone is incapable of overcoming sin and securing God's promises.

The Covenant Must Lead Us to Jesus

Israel's experience under the Mosaic covenant was intended to be an object lesson to us because Israel's story is humanity's story. It takes God's power and supernatural transformation in us to overcome sin, to enable us to live in relationship with Him, and to fulfill our calling. The Mosaic covenant revealed our predicament, but it was unable to deliver us. Therefore, the purpose of the law was to lead us to Jesus who can supernaturally deliver us:

> *Nevertheless knowing that a man is not justified by the works of the Law but through faith in Christ Jesus, even we have believed in Christ Jesus, so that we may be justified by faith in Christ and not by the works*

---

[6] See Joshua 7.

of the Law; since by the works of the Law no flesh will be justified. (Galatians 2:16 NASB)

Therefore the Law has become our tutor to lead us to Christ, so that we may be justified by faith. (3:24 NASB)

For the Law, since it has only a shadow of the good things to come and not the very form of things, can never, by the same sacrifices which they offer continually year by year, make perfect those who draw near. Otherwise, would they not have ceased to be offered, because the worshipers, having once been cleansed, would no longer have had consciousness of sins? But in those sacrifices there is a reminder of sins year by year. For it is impossible for the blood of bulls and goats to take away sins. (Hebrews 10:1–4 NASB)

By a new and living way which He inaugurated for us through the veil, that is, His flesh. . . . (v. 20 NASB)

This covenant did not simply disappear with the coming of Jesus. Jesus secured a new covenant, but there is a process by which Israel must transition from the Mosaic covenant to the new covenant. Until that transition happens, the nation remains subject to the terms of the covenant. As we proceed, we will see how the covenant continues to affect Israel, how it will be resolved by Jesus' return, and what role it plays in setting the stage for the end times.

THE DISCIPLINE OF THE COVENANT

The curses of the Mosaic covenant result in what we can call *the discipline of the covenant*. While the discipline of the Mosaic covenant is unique to Israel, Israel's story reveals God's nature and His character. *Therefore, God's discipline of Israel instructs us in the knowledge of God.*

God's discipline was not unique to Israel nor did it end with Jesus' first coming. Paul warned the Gentiles that Jesus' first coming has intensified God's judgment of the nations and set the stage for a coming day of judgment unlike any other day:

> "*Therefore having overlooked the times of ignorance, God is now declaring to men that all people everywhere should repent, because He has fixed a day in which He will judge the world in righteousness through a Man whom He has appointed, having furnished proof to all men by raising Him from the dead.*" (Acts 17:30–31 NASB)

> But because of your stubbornness and unrepentant heart you are storing up wrath for yourself in the day of wrath and revelation of the righteous judgment of God. (Romans 2:5 NASB)

God's judgment in the Old Testament was not limited to Israel. God also spoke severe words of judgment to the nations, often as a warning to them about resisting His redemptive purpose for Israel.[1] God warned the nations to not take advantage of Israel's discipline by trying to seize her inheritance. Edom in particular tried to take advantage of God's judgment and, as a result, came under severe judgment:

> "*Will I not on that day, declares the Lord, destroy the wise men out of Edom, and understanding out of Mount Esau? . . . But do not gloat*

---

[1] See Isaiah 34; Joel 3; Zechariah 14.

over the day of your brother in the day of his misfortune; do not rejoice over the people of Judah in the day of their ruin; do not boast in the day of distress. . . . For the day of the Lord is near upon all the nations. As you have done, it shall be done to you; your deeds shall return on your own head. . . . The house of Jacob shall be a fire, and the house of Joseph a flame, and the house of Esau stubble; they shall burn them and consume them, and there shall be no survivor for the house of Esau, for the Lord has spoken." (Obadiah 8, 12, 15, 18)

Because God's discipline plays a significant role in how He relates to Israel and the nations, we need to lay a basic foundation for how we approach the subject.

God Makes Himself Known in His Judgments

God reveals Himself in His judgments. Consider the words of Ezekiel:[2]

"My eye will show no pity nor will I spare. I will repay you according to your ways, while your abominations are in your midst; then you will know that I, the Lord, do the smiting." (Ezekiel 7:9 NASB)

"Your lewdness will be requited upon you, and you will bear the penalty of worshiping your idols; thus you will know that I am the Lord God." (23:49 NASB)

"Thus I will execute judgments on Egypt, And they will know that I am the Lord." (30:19 NASB)

"Then they will know that I am the Lord, when I make the land a desolation and a waste because of all their abominations which they have committed." (33:29 NASB)

---

[2] God repeatedly tells Ezekiel that Israel and the nations will know "I am the Lord," and the vast majority of those statements are in the context of His judgments. See Ezekiel 5:13, 15; 6:7, 10, 13–14; 7:4, 9, 27; 11:10, 12; 12:15–16, 20; 13:9, 14, 21, 23; 14:8; 15:7; 16:62; 17:21, 24; 20:7, 12, 20, 26, 38, 42, 44; 21:5; 22:16, 22; 23:49; 24:14, 24, 27; 25:5, 7, 11, 17; 26:6, 14; 28:22–24, 26; 29:6, 16, 21; 30:8, 12, 19, 25–26; 32:15; 33:29; 34:27, 30; 35:4, 9, 15; 36:11, 22–23, 36, 38; 37:6, 13, 28; 38:23; 39:6–7, 21–23, 28.

God does not judge for capricious or vindictive reasons. He judges for the sake of His name—to make Himself known:

"'Then you will know that I am the Lord when I have dealt with you for My name's sake, not according to your evil ways or according to your corrupt deeds, O house of Israel,' declares the Lord God." (Ezekiel 20:44 NASB)

"Therefore say to the house of Israel, 'Thus says the Lord God, "It is not for your sake, O house of Israel, that I am about to act, but for My holy name, which you have profaned among the nations where you went. I will vindicate the holiness of My great name which has been profaned among the nations, which you have profaned in their midst. Then the nations will know that I am the Lord," declares the Lord God, "when I prove Myself holy among you in their sight."'" (36:22–23 NASB)

God's primary concern in judgment is the greatness of His holy name. Biblically, God's judgments reveal His nature, His character, His beauty, and His glory.

Sin is more than the violation of arbitrary rules. Ultimately, it is the violation of a Person. This is why God compared Israel's sin to adultery.[3] Adultery in a marriage is not simply breaking a rule; it is the violation of another person. *Sin is personal not mechanical.* Sin against God is the violation of a Person who created us for intimate relationship. It destroys relationship with God just as adultery destroys a marriage. The incredible message of the Bible is that God—though violated by Israel and the nations—aggressively seeks to restore relationship with them.

When we sin, we make a statement about who God is. Sin is a statement we know better than God how to seek our own good and our own joy. When we reject His ways, we are challenging His character because His ways flow from who He is. Sin is a statement God is not perfectly good, and not truly acting in the best interest of creation. Our sin corrupts God's good creation and that violation of creation is a violation of God who formed creation for His joy and His purposes.

Because sin is an accusation against God, God must respond to the accusation against His goodness. He must demonstrate that He is good first and that His goodness is expressed in the way He relates to His creation. His

---

[3] See Deuteronomy 31:16; Ezekiel 16; 23:11; Hosea 1:2; Jeremiah 3:8-10;

judgments are an expression of how He feels about our corruption and violation of creation.

A judge reveals his goodness in the way he responds to crimes committed, and God is no different. The sentences a judge gives to criminals reveal what the judge values and how much he cares for the people who have been violated. The glory of a judge is that he demonstrates what is beautiful and true by his judgments of what is wicked. It is the same with God. *His judgments reveal His value for His holiness and His care for His creation which is violated by our sin.* Therefore, He does not apologize for His judgments.

When we sin, not only are we making a statement that we know good better than God, we are also making a statement that what God defines as evil is not truly evil. Our presumption that God will not respond to our sin is a statement that God's laws are not worth enforcing and, therefore, not true and valuable expressions of His goodness.

You can always tell what is important to a parent by what they enforce. Children quickly learn the real rules of a house by observing what the parents enforce and what they do not enforce. Rules that are not enforced are essentially not real. When we sin as though God will never respond, we are saying we do not believe God's law is valuable enough for Him to respond. It is a challenge to the goodness and value of His character.

However, God is not some sort of cosmic absent father. He is intricately involved in His creation. He responds to wickedness. He takes the time and effort to defend His precepts as right and true. He takes the time necessary to demonstrate the value of His just requirements.

If God did not judge violations of His law, effectively, it would be an agreement with rebellious humans that sin is "not that bad" because it is not worth His effort to enforce. However, because His laws are an expression of His nature, and our sin is an accusation against that nature, He must respond to our violations of His law to demonstrate the value of who He is as it is expressed in His good laws.

We tend to be uncomfortable with His judgments because we are so comfortable with sin. Sin is familiar to us. It is reasonable to us. It may seem bad, but it doesn't seem *that bad*. In reality, it is overt rebellion that maligns God's good nature. It is a public challenge to His goodness, and when God responds in His judgment, He instructs the nations in His righteousness:

For when the earth experiences Your judgments the inhabitants of the world learn righteousness. (Isaiah 26:9 NASB)

In His judgments, God displays the glory of His name and warns the nations of a much greater eternal judgment coming for those who persist in their sin. Therefore, His judgments are a kind gift to the nations.

The Redemptive Nature of God's Judgments

We tend to think of God's judgments primarily in terms of the punishment they inflict, but they are also redemptive. *When God releases His judgments for His name's sake, the natural result is the redemption and restoration of creation.* The ultimate outcome of judgment is not death, but life.

God's name is made great both in His judgments and in the redemption that follows His judgments:

Then the nations that are left round about you will know that I, the Lord, have rebuilt the ruined places and planted that which was desolate; I, the Lord, have spoken and will do it. (Ezekiel 36:36 NASB)

Then you will know that I am the Lord, when I have opened your graves and caused you to come up out of your graves, My people. (37:13 NASB)

And the nations will know that I am the Lord who sanctifies Israel, when My sanctuary is in their midst forever. (v. 28 NASB)

The redemptive outcome of God's judgments is another demonstration of the greatness of His character. We tend to think God is most glorified in His ability to redeem, but He is glorified both in His judgments and His salvation. Both are demonstrations of His nature. They are not at odds. They are both part of the goodness of God towards His creation. Real life—true life—is the result of God's judgments. He must judge what is false and enslaving that we may experience true life.

When God seeks His own glory, it becomes the means of our salvation.

God's zeal for His name is at the root of His relationship with Israel and with the nations. God will ultimately demonstrate His zeal for

His own name by bringing a people to salvation through those judgments.

The Cross—The Ultimate Revelation of God's Judgments

The cross is the ultimate demonstration of the nature of God's judgments. It reveals the certainty of God's judgments, the perfection of God's judgments, and the redemptive nature of His judgments.

First, the cross reveals God's judgment is certain.[4] There is no escape from it. God's goodness required Him to respond to our wickedness. It was unavoidable. A righteous God had to demonstrate His goodness through judgment. Jesus bore the wrath of God because there was no other way.[5]

Second, the cross reveals God's judgment is perfect. *God's judgments are so perfect that He was willing to undergo His own judgments.* This is the ultimate indicator of how right and perfect God's judgments are. He did not apologize for His wrath. Instead, He willingly endured His own perfect wrath for the sake of His creation.

Finally, the cross demonstrates God's judgment is ultimately redemptive. He is so good His judgments result in life for those in agreement with Him. Just as God's judgment of Jesus secured redemption for millions, His judgments will ultimately bring about the redemption of the cosmos.

The cross graphically demonstrates that God's wrath becomes the cradle of his mercy.

There is no other name under heaven by which we can be saved because salvation must come through God's judgments.[6] If we agree with His judgments, we can receive mercy through Jesus. If we reject the goodness of His judgments, those judgments will justly punish us among the rebellious who contribute to the destruction of creation.

Jesus' suffering on the cross answers every accusation against God's judgment. His willing suffering demonstrates the perfection of God's

---

[4] See John 3:16-18.

[5] See Isaiah 53:6; Romans 5:9; 2 Corinthians 5:21.

[6] See John 3:36; 14:6; Acts 4:12; 10:42-43; 1 Corinthians 3:11; 1 Timothy 2:5-6; 1 John 5:11-12.

judgments, and His offer of redemption reveals the redemptive nature of God's judgments.

The Vengeance of the Covenant

God's judgments are described as the *vengeance of the covenant*.[7] God's goodness causes Him to respond to the blasphemy of His name with vengeance. His vengeance results in great good for His people.

Creation flourishes when God expresses His zeal for His own glory. This is a key difference between God and man. When men seek their own glory, other humans suffer. When God seeks and reveals His glory, all of creation benefits. God's bold pursuit of His own glory is not selfish; it is the kindest thing He can do.

When God glorifies Himself in judgment, He answers the rage— what we call *sin*—against Him.

Those who embrace and promote sin threaten God's people by promoting the things that destroy man's calling. Therefore, when God acts in judgment, He preserves His people. In this way, the Mosaic covenant executed punishment against those who threatened the calling of the people in order to steward the people for a coming day of salvation. God's discipline is not His final word, and so He remained fully committed to Israel's future even when she broke covenant:

> *"Yet for all that, when they are in the land of their enemies, I will not spurn them, neither will I abhor them so as to destroy them utterly and break my covenant with them, for I am the Lord their God. But I will for their sake remember the covenant with their forefathers, whom I brought out of the land of Egypt in the sight of the nations, that I might be their God: I am the Lord." (Leviticus 26:44–45)*

God's Loving Discipline of Israel

We are usually uncomfortable with God's judgments because we lack a revelation of the greatness of God and His name. When we esteem a person, we are naturally enraged when their name is maligned. *The greater revelation we have of the greatness of God, the greater agreement we will have regarding God and His judgments.*

Some are uncomfortable with God's judgments because they have experienced ungodly discipline by flawed fathers. But God is not like

---

[7] See Leviticus 26:25.

that. He is patient. He does not act out of vindictive rage. He is a good Father who acts for our good. His discipline is an expression of our sonship and His love for us.[8]

Israel's time in the wilderness reveals God's tender concern in His judgments. The people rebelled repeatedly against Him, complained constantly, and even worshipped a golden calf. Because of their rebellion, an entire generation was not allowed to enter the Promised Land.[9]

The time Israel spent in the wilderness seems like a tragic story because of the people's sin and God's judgments. However, when God referred to Israel's wandering in the wilderness, He referred to it as a time of love rather than as a time of rebellion. He described it the way a man would describe the love of the woman he was going to marry:[10]

> *"Go and proclaim in the hearing of Jerusalem, Thus says the Lord, 'I remember the devotion of your youth, your love as a bride, how you followed me in the wilderness, in a land not sown.'" (Jeremiah 2:2)*

God's language in Jeremiah 2 is surprising, especially when we compare it to the stories about Israel's time in the wilderness. It gives us tremendous insight into God's emotions, His mercy, His patience, and His purposes for His judgments. His love for Israel caused Him to view Israel's rebellious beginnings with deep affection.

God's assessment of Israel's time in the wilderness reminds us what happens when we ask parents about their children's early years. The parents of older children will typically describe those early years with tenderness and affection. They will mention the cute and endearing things their children did. They will pull out pictures and boast about their children's milestones.

In reality, those were years when the parents were exhausted, tired, frustrated, and frequently had to discipline and restrain their children. However, the memories that are highlighted by the parents reveal what they truly think about their children. Even if hard work and discipline are necessary, parents have positive memories of their children's early years because their kids are *their* kids. Parents discipline and struggle

---

[8] See Hebrews 12:6–8.

[9] See Leviticus 10:2; Numbers 16:30–35; 21:6; Deuteronomy 1:35.

[10] See also Hosea 2:15.

with their children because they care for their children, not because they are disgusted with them.

God often evaluates things differently than we do because He knows the outcome, just as a parent evaluates childish rebellion and immaturity in light of the child's future maturity. God cannot overlook sin, and so His discipline is serious and real. At the same time, He is not a vindictive tyrant waiting to punish and cut off His people. He is a loving Father laboring to bring a people to maturity.

God does not shy away from His judgments, but He also makes it clear that His end is mercy. *The same mercy that has saved every believer is going to one day save Israel.*

God Disciplines His Children

God's discipline may seem severe, but it is ultimately a display of His righteousness for our good. In His discipline, God displays His glory, the seriousness of sin, His tender concern for us, and His commitment to mature us.

God's discipline is so perfect His own Son was matured by it:

> *Although He was a Son, He learned obedience from the things which He suffered. (Hebrews 5:8 NASB)*

If we do not understand God's discipline of Israel, we will struggle to understand His discipline in our own lives.

> *And you have forgotten the exhortation which is addressed to you as sons, "My son, do not regard lightly the discipline of the Lord, nor faint when you are reproved by Him; for those whom the Lord loves He disciplines, and He scourges every son whom He receives." It is for discipline that you endure; God deals with you as with sons; for what son is there whom his father does not discipline? But if you are without discipline, of which all have become partakers, then you are illegitimate children and not sons. Furthermore, we had earthly fathers to discipline us, and we respected them; shall we not much rather be subject to the Father of spirits, and live? For they disciplined us for a short time as seemed best to them, but He disciplines us for our good, so that we may share His holiness. All discipline for the moment seems not to be joyful, but sorrowful; yet to those who have been trained by it, afterwards it yields the peaceful fruit of righteousness. (Hebrews 12:5–11 NASB)*

God's discipline is a statement of His involvement. As sons and daughters of God, we experience His discipline as part of His process to bring us to maturity.[11] God refers to Israel as His firstborn son among the nations,[12] and God disciplines all His sons whether they are individuals or nations. Lack of discipline is a sign we are not true children of His:

> *But if you are without discipline, of which all have become partakers, then you are illegitimate children and not sons. (Hebrews 12:8 NASB)*

God's Discipline is a Sign of His Commitment

God's judgments preserve His unique purposes for Israel. They are not a sign of His rejection of Israel, but a sign of His unique relationship to her. God disciplines Israel so she will ultimately become the saved nation He has destined her to be.

When God delays judgment, sin and wickedness increase. Therefore, His judgments are an expression of mercy because they stop wickedness before it can escalate and do even more harm. *God's punishments are a demonstration of His value for righteousness and his hatred for sin.* We do the same when we enact punishments to deter others from committing a crime and to make a statement of the seriousness of a crime.

God is patient and long-suffering in His judgments. He sends prophets for decades and, in some cases, centuries to warn the people before He releases His judgments. He is not eager to discipline for the sake of discipline. He is quick to relent when there is repentance. God sent Israel into captivity for her rebellion, yet He refused to cut Israel off permanently.[13] He responded to Israel's broken covenant by promising a new covenant that would resolve the broken covenant.[14] God's mercy towards Israel throughout her history reveals His nature and character.

God's judgments on Israel have never been arbitrary. They are a result of the covenant, and God uses them to protect Israel's calling. They protect Israel's calling in two ways. First, they reveal the holiness

---

[11] See Romans 8:18–19.

[12] See Exodus 4:22; Hosea 11:1.

[13] See Jeremiah 31:35–37.

[14] See Jeremiah 31:31–32; Hebrews 8.

and greatness of God. This revelation is Israel's greatest need because this revelation will finally provoke Israel to turn to God for His salvation.

Second, God's judgments cut Israel off from the sin that seduces her. The sinful ways of the nations have always been attractive to Israel; therefore, God uses the nations in His judgments to show Israel that the way of the nations results in death, destruction, and oppression.

Israel's story is a graphic warning that the sin we find so attractive ends in death.

THE TENSION OF THE COVENANTS

The Mosaic covenant offered a demonstration of mercy in the sacrificial system, but it was not capable of providing a final, complete atonement and, therefore, unable to secure the nation's blessings. As Israel's history unfolded, Israel's situation seemed increasingly dire.

The promises of the Abrahamic covenant and the curses of the Mosaic covenant created a profound tension. On one hand, God must fulfill His promises to Abraham, or He is a liar, and His entire redemptive plan collapses because He is unable to do what He said He would do. On the other hand, the curses of the Mosaic covenant create a seemingly impossible barrier to God fulfilling His promises.

For example, the Abrahamic covenant promises Israel will be a righteous nation in the earth and inherit the land promised to Abraham. However, the curse for disobedience under the terms of the Mosaic covenant includes her humiliation in the sight of the nations and her loss of the land:

> *"And I myself will devastate the land, so that your enemies who settle in it shall be appalled at it. And I will scatter you among the nations, and I will unsheathe the sword after you, and your land shall be a desolation, and your cities shall be a waste." (Leviticus 26:32–33)*

> *"And the Lord will scatter you among all peoples, from one end of the earth to the other, and there you shall serve other gods of wood and stone, which neither you nor your fathers have known. And among these nations you shall find no respite, and there shall be no resting place for the sole of your foot, but the Lord will give you there a trembling heart and failing eyes and a languishing soul." (Deuteronomy 28:64–65)*

Under the terms of the covenant, the entire nation has to be righteous to eliminate the possibility of judgment because God made the covenant corporately. When we survey Israel's history and her failures, we are left wondering: How can an entire nation ever be completely righteous before God with no threat of judgment? Yet, this is what Abraham was promised.

God has given Himself an impossible mission: He must fulfill all His promises while somehow resolving the curses that prevent the fulfillment of those promises.

Understanding God's plan to resolve Israel's national crisis due to the terms of the Mosaic covenant is critical to understanding God's work in the nations and God's plan with Israel in the end times. *In the same way that the end times are driven by the fulfillment of God's promises to Abraham, they are also driven by the resolution of the Mosaic covenant.* The terms of the Mosaic covenant and God's surprising plan to resolve it are two of the biggest factors affecting why the end times unfold the way they do.

This covenantal tension and God's plan to resolve it is a picture of our own human predicament. Humanity, like Israel, has been called by God and given an assignment. Humans, like Israel, have failed to live up to God's requirements and need a redemption that only God can provide. The great question for Israel—and all humanity—is this: How will God bring deliverance while also being true to His character and His judgments?

Israel's experience under the Mosaic covenant is God's statement to us about our own condition. Not only are we incapable of true outward righteousness, Jesus went even further and exposed the deeper issue: Our outward sin is the result of something far more serious—inward sin.[1] Jesus forever shattered our delusion of our own ability to be "good" people. *There is no human solution for Israel or the nations.* Israel's failure is our failure, and Israel's hope is our hope.

This tension is one of the major tensions in the Old Testament, and it sets the context for the New Testament and a Messiah who will deliver Israel from the curses of the covenant.

The Prophets and the Covenants

Jeremiah predicted this covenant tension would be resolved:

---

[1] See Matthew 5:21–37.

"Behold, the days are coming, declares the Lord, when I will make a new covenant with the house of Israel and the house of Judah, not like the covenant that I made with their fathers on the day when I took them by the hand to bring them out of the land of Egypt, my covenant that they broke, though I was their husband, declares the Lord." (Jeremiah 31:31– 32)

Jeremiah predicted a day would come when Israel received her promises, but it would require a covenant that is not like the one made at Sinai. *One of the great mysteries of the Old Testament is how God will accomplish Israel's deliverance and transition the nation from the Mosaic covenant to the new covenant.*

The tension between Abraham's promises and the Mosaic covenant is the foundation of the prophets, and their prophecies of judgment and of salvation were rooted in the covenants. *God gave the prophets specific details, but most of their prophecies were an application of the terms of the covenant at a specific point in time looking forward to a future resolution.*

For example, when the prophet Daniel interceded for Israel after the Babylonians destroyed Jerusalem, he recognized that this judgment was a result of the covenant:

To the Lord our God belong mercy and forgiveness, for we have rebelled against him and have not obeyed the voice of the Lord our God by walking in his laws, which he set before us by his servants the prophets. All Israel has transgressed your law and turned aside, refusing to obey your voice. And the curse and oath that are written in the Law of Moses the servant of God have been poured out upon us, because we have sinned against him. He has confirmed his words, which he spoke against us and against our rulers who ruled us, by bringing upon us a great calamity. For under the whole heaven there has not been done anything like what has been done against Jerusalem. As it is written in the Law of Moses, all this calamity has come upon us; yet we have not entreated the favor of the Lord our God, turning from our iniquities and gaining insight by your truth. Therefore the Lord has kept ready the calamity and has brought it upon us, for the Lord our God is righteous in all the works that he has done, and we have not obeyed his voice. (9:9–14)

Daniel, like all the prophets, recognized the covenants drive Israel's story, Israel's judgment, and Israel's salvation. Daniel interceded for mercy because he was confident the promises of God would provide a way of escape for the nation from the endless cycle of judgment:

O Lord, according to all your righteous acts, let your anger and your wrath turn away from your city Jerusalem, your holy hill, because for our sins, and for the iniquities of our fathers, Jerusalem and your people have become a byword among all who are around us. Now therefore, O our God, listen to the prayer of your servant and to his pleas for mercy, and for your own sake, O Lord, make your face to shine upon your sanctuary, which is desolate. O my God, incline your ear and hear. Open your eyes and see our desolations, and the city that is called by your name. For we do not present our pleas before you because of our righteousness, but because of your great mercy. O Lord, hear; O Lord, forgive. O Lord, pay attention and act. Delay not, for your own sake, O my God, because your city and your people are called by your name. (9:16–19)

The prophets made sudden and dramatic shifts between graphic proclamations of God's judgments and bold predictions of God's deliverance. Salvation and judgment appeared in the same passages. God's terrifying wrath and tender love could appear in the same oracle. This was because the prophets and their prophecies were anchored in the covenants.

They prophesied out of the covenant made with Abraham, which promised ultimate blessing, and out of the Mosaic covenant, which required God's judgments. The prophets seem to make sudden leaps between two very different themes, but once we realize they are caught in the tension of the covenants, their oracles make sense. The prophets did not know how God would resolve this tension, but they knew He would.

Jeremiah 30 is an excellent example of this kind of prophecy. It begins with a terrifying description of Israel's judgment. It describes screams of terror and men in anguish because of an incomprehensible day of trouble. Then the prophecy suddenly shifts to a prediction of God's salvation and deliverance:

"Thus says the Lord: We have heard a cry of panic, of terror, and no peace. Ask now, and see, can a man bear a child? Why then do I see every man with his hands on his stomach like a woman in labor? Why has every face turned pale? Alas! That day is so great there is none like

it; it is a time of distress for Jacob; yet he shall be saved out of it. And it shall come to pass in that day, declares the Lord of hosts, that I will break his yoke from off your neck, and I will burst your bonds, and foreigners shall no more make a servant of him. But they shall serve the Lord their God and David their king, whom I will raise up for them. Then fear not, O Jacob my servant, declares the Lord, nor be dismayed, O Israel; for behold, I will save you from far away, and your offspring from the land of their captivity. Jacob shall return and have quiet and ease, and none shall make him afraid. For I am with you to save you, declares the Lord; I will make a full end of all the nations among whom I scattered you, but of you I will not make a full end. I will discipline you in just measure, and I will by no means leave you unpunished." (vv. 5–11)

Prophecies like this expose one of the serious issues with the belief that the church has superseded Israel as the covenant people and, as a result, promises made to Israel in the Old Testament should be applied to the church without any specific application for Israel (this is commonly known as *supersessionism*).[2] When the Old Testament prophets address Israel in their oracles, they apply the covenants to Israel and predict both judgment *and* deliverance for Israel. Supersessionism divides these prophecies so that the prophecies of judgment apply primarily to Israel and the prophecies of salvation apply primarily to the church. This is inconsistent and adds confusion to the prophets' oracles.

We have to apply prophecy consistently. Either the judgment and the salvation the prophets predict for Israel have a specific application for Israel, or they do not have a specific meaning for Israel. Both the judgment and the promises are directed to Israel, so we must define Israel consistently. This does not mean there cannot be secondary applications of these prophecies to the nations, but we have to be consistent on how we interpret Israel in these passages.

These prophecies also have a specific application to Israel because the judgments prophesied are based on the Mosaic covenant—a covenant uniquely made with Israel and not the nations. Therefore, the

---

[2] Supercessionism is sometimes referred to as *fulfillment theology* by its supporters and *replacement theology* by its critics.

judgment must be applied first of all to Israel. Virtually all biblical scholars agree on this point when it relates to Israel's judgment. However, the promise of salvation must also be applied first of all to Israel, and this is where there has been inconsistency.

This inconsistency is perhaps most obvious in how some scholars interpret the destruction of Jerusalem in AD 70. Supersessionism teaches that the destruction of Jerusalem in AD 70 and the subsequent Diaspora were divine judgments on unbelieving Israel and essentially the end of God's unique dealings with her. While AD 70 should be understood as a judgment on unbelieving Israel, the idea that Israel's story ends in judgment violates the consistent interpretation of the prophets who predicted Israel's judgments must end with Israel's salvation.

Some say Israel's salvation is accomplished as part of the salvation of the nations, but this is an inconsistent interpretation of the prophets. Just as there are specific judgments for Israel according to the terms of the covenant, the covenants also include a specific salvation for Israel.

God's Commitment to Resolve the Tension

Though Exodus, Leviticus, and Deuteronomy do not give us much information on how God will resolve the curses of the covenant, they do give us a hint that God is going to find a way to keep covenant with Israel. Though Israel will fail, Abraham's covenant provides a basis for God's unbreakable commitment to her.

> *"Then [when the people repent] I will remember my covenant with Jacob, and I will remember my covenant with Isaac and my covenant with Abraham, and I will remember the land. . . . Yet for all that, when they are in the land of their enemies, I will not spurn them, neither will I abhor them so as to destroy them utterly and break my covenant with them, for I am the Lord their God. But I will for their sake remember the covenant with their forefathers, whom I brought out of the land of Egypt in the sight of the nations, that I might be their God: I am the Lord." (Leviticus 26:42, 44–45)*

While Israel worshipped the golden calf, Moses appealed to God's covenantal promises and asked God to give Israel mercy rather than the judgment she deserved. Moses made this bold request at the very moment Israel was worshipping a false idol because he knew the strength of God's covenantal commitment to Israel.

And the Lord said to Moses, "Go down, for your people, whom you brought up out of the land of Egypt, have corrupted themselves. They have turned aside quickly out of the way that I commanded them. They have made for themselves a golden calf and have worshiped it and sacrificed to it and said, 'These are your gods, O Israel, who brought you up out of the land of Egypt!'" And the Lord said to Moses, "I have seen this people, and behold, it is a stiff-necked people. Now therefore let me alone, that my wrath may burn hot against them and I may consume them, in order that I may make a great nation of you." But Moses implored the Lord his God and said, "O Lord, why does your wrath burn hot against your people, whom you have brought out of the land of Egypt with great power and with a mighty hand? . . . . Remember Abraham, Isaac, and Israel, your servants, to whom you swore by your own self, and said to them, 'I will multiply your offspring as the stars of heaven, and all this land that I have promised I will give to your offspring, and they shall inherit it forever.'" (Exodus 32:7–11, 13)

God's Resolution: The New Covenant

God displays His glory both in His judgments and His salvation. The Mosaic covenant set a context for God to display His glory in His judgments, but He must also display His glory in His salvation. The Mosaic covenant cannot reveal the glory of God's salvation; therefore, Israel must be transitioned to what Jeremiah called the *new covenant*.[3]

It is a covenant not like the one made at Sinai because it is secured by God's righteousness instead of the nation's obedience. Therefore, it is capable of fully saving Israel.

"Behold, the days are coming, declares the Lord, when I will make a new covenant with the house of Israel and the house of Judah, not like the covenant that I made with their fathers on the day when I took them by the hand to bring them out of the land of Egypt, my covenant that they broke, though I was their husband, declares the Lord. For this is the covenant that I will make with the house of Israel after those days, declares the Lord: I will put my law within them, and I will write it on

---

[3] See Jeremiah 31:31–34.

their hearts. And I will be their God, and they shall be my people. And no longer shall each one teach his neighbor and each his brother, saying, 'Know the Lord,' for they shall all know me, from the least of them to the greatest, declares the Lord. For I will forgive their iniquity, and I will remember their sin no more." (Jeremiah 31:31–34)

Ezekiel referred to this covenant as an everlasting covenant:

"Yet I will remember my covenant with you in the days of your youth, and I will establish for you an everlasting covenant." (Ezekiel 16:60)

"I will take you from the nations and gather you from all the countries and bring you into your own land. I will sprinkle clean water on you, and you shall be clean from all your uncleannesses, and from all your idols I will cleanse you. And I will give you a new heart, and a new spirit I will put within you. And I will remove the heart of stone from your flesh and give you a heart of flesh. And I will put my Spirit within you, and cause you to walk in my statutes and be careful to obey my rules. You shall dwell in the land that I gave to your fathers, and you shall be my people, and I will be your God." (36:24–28)

Hosea also described a day when God would make covenant with Israel again:

"And I will make for them a covenant on that day with the beasts of the field, the birds of the heavens, and the creeping things of the ground. And I will abolish the bow, the sword, and war from the land, and I will make you lie down in safety. And I will betroth you to me forever. I will betroth you to me in righteousness and in justice, in steadfast love and in mercy. I will betroth you to me in faithfulness. And you shall know the Lord." (Hosea 2:18–20)

The book of Hebrews quoted Jeremiah's prediction of a new covenant:

But as it is, Christ has obtained a ministry that is as much more excellent than the old as the covenant he mediates is better, since it is enacted on better promises. For if that first covenant had been faultless, there would have been no occasion to look for a second. For he finds fault with them when he says: "Behold, the days are coming, declares the Lord, when I will establish a new covenant with the house of Israel and with the house of Judah, not like the covenant that I made with their fathers on the day when I took them by the hand to bring them out of the land of Egypt. For they did not continue in my covenant, and so I showed no concern for them, declares the Lord. For this is the covenant that I will make with the house of Israel after those days, declares the Lord: I will put my laws into their minds, and write them on their hearts, and I will be their God, and they shall be my people. And they shall not teach, each one his neighbor and each one his brother, saying, 'Know the Lord,' for they shall all know me, from the least of them to the greatest. For I will be merciful toward their iniquities, and I will remember their sins no more." In speaking of a new covenant, he makes the first one obsolete. And what is becoming obsolete and growing old is ready to vanish away. (8:6–13)

Since the Mosaic covenant cannot deliver because the outcome is determined by the righteousness of human beings, God has made provision for Israel through a new covenant. *Notice the author of Hebrews does not redefine the terms* Israel *and* Judah. The new covenant provides for the salvation of the nations, but it also must save Israel and Judah in order to resolve Israel's crisis and set the stage for the fulfillment of the promises.

The new covenant was the hope of Israel in the Old Testament. It is the promise that God is going to resolve an impossible situation. The great question was how this new covenant would come and how the Mosaic covenant would be resolved. The New Testament answers that question. The new covenant came with the suffering, death, and resurrection of Jesus.

Now that the new covenant has arrived, we discover God's plan to bring Israel, as a nation, out of the Mosaic covenant and into the new covenant. In Romans 7, Paul described how a shift of covenant happens:

Or do you not know, brothers—for I am speaking to those who know the law—that the law is binding on a person only as long as he lives? For a married woman is bound by law to her husband while he lives, but if her husband dies she is released from the law of marriage. Accordingly, she will be called an adulteress if she lives with another man while her husband is alive. But if her husband dies, she is free from that law, and if she marries another man she is not an adulteress. Likewise, my brothers, you also have died to the law through the body of Christ, so that you may belong to another, to him who has been raised from the dead, in order that we may bear fruit for God. (vv. 1–4)

In order to break a marriage covenant, one of the covenant partners must die. Paul used this analogy because God referred to what happened at Sinai as the initiation of a marriage covenant.

"For your Maker is your husband, the Lord of hosts is his name; and the Holy One of Israel is your Redeemer, the God of the whole earth he is called." (Isaiah 54:5)

"Go and proclaim in the hearing of Jerusalem, Thus says the Lord, 'I remember the devotion of your youth, your love as a bride, how you followed me in the wilderness, in a land not sown.'" (Jeremiah 2:2)

"When I passed by you again and saw you, behold, you were at the age for love, and I spread the corner of my garment over you and covered your nakedness; I made my vow to you and entered into a covenant with you, declares the Lord God, and you became mine." (Ezekiel 16:8)

Romans 7 describes what must happen to individuals, but also what must happen to Israel as a nation. The entire nation must pass through a "death" to be released from the Mosaic covenant and enter into a new covenant. Paul explained that the death of Jesus is the means of that transition because He died on behalf of Israel.[4] When we come into Him, we are identified with His death and are joined to Him. Therefore, through Jesus' death, Israel can enter into a new covenant and escape the old one.

God's commitment to Israel remains, but the covenant through which He relates to her must change in order for Him to be joined to her forever. *God brings resolution to the covenant crisis in Jesus, but Israel must enter into this resolution as a nation for the effects of the Mosaic covenant to permanently pass away.* Israel's transition from the Mosaic covenant to the new covenant is one of the main themes of the end times.

---

[4] See John 11:50–52.

Discipline, Despair, and Deliverance

As Moses gave the covenant, he warned the people that they would not be able to keep it and, as a result, would experience the discipline, or curses, of the covenant:

> *All these curses shall come upon you and pursue you and overtake you till you are destroyed, because you did not obey the voice of the Lord your God, to keep his commandments and his statutes that he commanded you. They shall be a sign and a wonder against you and your offspring forever. (Deuteronomy 28:45–46)*

On one hand, the requirements of the law are good. On another hand, humans cannot keep the law. Even when blessings are offered for obedience, and very real threats apply for disobedience, man still cannot secure God's blessings in his own strength because he is simply unable to live in the way that is required by God's righteousness. Paul identified the core issue:

> *For all have sinned and fall short of the glory of God. (Romans 3:23)*

Israel's failure sends a clear message: We cannot secure our own destiny. We need someone to come and save us to secure it. The frustration inherent in the Mosaic law is designed to cause us to look outside ourselves for salvation—in fact, to look to God. In this way, the law serves as a "tutor" or teacher who brings us to Jesus:

> *But before faith came, we were kept in custody under the law, being shut up to the faith which was later to be revealed. Therefore the Law has become our tutor to lead us to Christ, so that we may be justified by faith. But now that faith has come, we are no longer under a tutor. (Galatians 3:23–25 NASB)*

Jesus emphasized how serious the situation was in the Sermon on the Mount when He addressed the core issue: inward sin. If a man does not commit adultery, the desire for it is in his mind and heart. If a man does not murder, anger still fills His heart. Even if Israel could keep the external law, the Jewish people could never cleanse their hearts and live in true righteousness because the sin, the ultimate source of rebellion against God, was constantly brewing inside each individual.

In order to fulfill His promises, God not only has to deliver Israel, He has to do something to deal with the root of sin and rebellion in her people. Sin is like a dog inside a cage. We can try to put the dog in the cage, but its bark reminds us it is there and is liable at any time to find a way out of the cage. Until this inward sin is dealt with, neither Israel nor the nations can permanently possess their inheritance.

The Cycle That Must End

Israel has experienced a measure of God's blessing and promises throughout history. From the Exodus onward, Israel has experienced God's favor in a way that is completely unique among the nations. At the same time, the discipline of the covenant is also one of the major factors that has defined Israel's history.[5]

In the book of Joshua, Achan's sin in the conquest of Jericho affected the entire nation. It was a warning to Israel that individual sin leads to national judgment. In the book of Judges, Israel repeatedly fell into sin and provoked God's judgments which resulted in her being under some form of foreign military oppression. However, when the nation responded and repented, God restored Israel. The book of Judges describes repeated cycles of judgment and deliverance, and they serve as a prediction of Israel's future.

Israel's sin provokes God's judgments, which involve harassment by the nations. However, when Israel repents, God will mercifully restore her. In a very real sense, this is a summary of Israel's history.

As Israel grew and matured as a nation, the same story unfolded. God was patient.[6] He sent prophets to warn the nation, but eventually Israel's sin provoked the curses of the covenant. It happened first to the northern half of Israel which was invaded and carried away by Assyria. A little over a century later, the southern half of Israel was invaded by Babylon. This invasion was even more serious because it involved the city of Jerusalem. The nation suffered unspeakable agony as Nebuchadnezzar ransacked the city, destroyed the temple, and carried away most of the population as exiles. Once again, Israel suffered the curses of the covenant.

---

[5] Biblically, discipline is a sign of sonship, and God's discipline of Israel is evidence of Israel's unique calling. See Hebrews 12:6–8.

[6] See Exodus 34:6.

When Jerusalem was destroyed, Israel's future appeared to be hopeless. However, just seventy years after the fall of Jerusalem, a remnant from Babylon began returning to Jerusalem, and a project to rebuild the temple began. The Babylonian invasion was not the end of Israel's story. God was going to preserve Israel in spite of her judgments.[7] He still remembered His promises, and prophets like Zechariah declared Israel's ultimate salvation.

In the following centuries, Israel struggled to establish herself in the land. Tragically, the nation drifted away from God's commands. Even more tragically, Israel refused her Messiah when He came and walked among her. In mercy, God poured out the Holy Spirit on the apostles and empowered the church to preach in Jerusalem and Judea for four decades to call the nation to repentance. Many did turn to God in repentance, even a number of the priests,[8] but the nation itself did not repent, and tragedy struck in AD 70. Jerusalem was taken, the temple was destroyed, and Israel was scattered into the nations due to the curses of the covenant.

For nearly two thousand years, there was no large-scale return to the land. However, God did not forget His covenant with Israel, and in the twentieth century God began regathering Israel again. In 1948, the nations were shocked by an impossible event: Israel emerged again as a sovereign nation. God regathered Israel in His mercy and, in the process, made a statement to the nations that He has not forgotten His promises to Israel.

Though He has gathered Israel in mercy, the covenant must still be resolved. Until the nation is saved, it will again experience the discipline of the covenant. *That discipline is designed to provoke her to cry out for salvation.* Israel remains subject to cycles of discipline, regathering with a hope of restoration, and discipline again until something resolves the threat of the covenant against the nation. As long as Israel trusts in her own strength to fulfill the covenant and secure her future, this cycle will continue.

---

[7] See Jeremiah 31:35–37; 33:14–26.

[8] See Acts 6:7.

A Corporate Romans 7 Struggle

Paul's personal experience—the agony of not being able to do the good that he wanted to do and instead doing the evil that he did not want to do—describes Israel's corporate history:

> For what I am doing, I do not understand; for I am not practicing what I would like to do, but I am doing the very thing I hate. But if I do the very thing I do not want to do, I agree with the Law, confessing that the Law is good. So now, no longer am I the one doing it, but sin which dwells in me. For I know that nothing good dwells in me, that is, in my flesh; for the willing is present in me, but the doing of the good is not. For the good that I want, I do not do, but I practice the very evil that I do not want. But if I am doing the very thing I do not want, I am no longer the one doing it, but sin which dwells in me. (Romans 7:15–20 NASB)

The sin in Paul's own heart kept him from being obedient to God's good law. The issue was not the law; it was Paul. This is the essence of the human struggle. We are trapped in a "body of death" and need deliverance. Paul's experience as an individual reflects Israel's experience as a nation. *The covenant Israel made at Sinai put Israel into a corporate Romans 7 experience.*

Israel was given a good law but was unable to keep God's law and, therefore, has become subject to the curses of that law and constantly in danger of judgment. Even Israel's greatest heroes, like King David, had serious violations of the law. Therefore, Israel needs a deliverer to end that cycle. That deliverer is Jesus, and the cycle will continue until the nations come into Jesus.

Paul's passionate plea must become Israel's plea so that Paul's salvation will become Israel's salvation:

> Wretched man that I am! Who will set me free from the body of this death? Thanks be to God through Jesus Christ our Lord! So then, on the one hand I myself with my mind am serving the law of God, but on the other, with my flesh the law of sin. Therefore there is now no condemnation for those who are in Christ Jesus. For the law of the Spirit of life in Christ Jesus has set you free from the law of sin and of death. (Romans 7:24–8:2 NASB)

Jacob only became Israel when Jacob wrestled with God and God emptied Jacob of his strength by putting his hip out of socket.[9] This is a picture of what happens when we come to Jesus. We come to the end of our strength, and we call on God for His salvation and trust in His strength. *Like her father Jacob, Israel must corporately come to a place where the nation has no confidence in her own strength and cries out to God for His salvation on His terms, secured by His ability.*

The Ongoing Effect of the Law

To fully understand the Mosaic covenant, we have to understand both how it passes away and how it continues to affect our world. The redemptive work of the cross is the only way the requirements of covenant pass away. Jesus alone provides an end to the Mosaic covenant:

> *For Christ is the end of the law for righteousness to everyone who believes. . . . For the Scripture says, "Everyone who believes in him will not be put to shame." (Romans 10:4, 11)*

Paul frequently used the phrase *the law* to refer to the Mosaic covenant. Now, notice carefully what Paul said. Jesus is the end of the law for "everyone who believes." Only those who believe in Him will not be put to shame—*only those who are in Jesus who are freed from the condemnation of the law and the curses of the covenant.* Therefore, the law is a "guardian" (or "tutor") designed by God to bring us to Christ:

> *So then, the law was our guardian until Christ came, in order that we might be justified by faith. But now that faith has come, we are no longer under a guardian, for in Christ Jesus you are all sons of God, through faith. (Galatians 3:24–26)*

In the same way a guardian prepares a minor for adulthood, the law prepares us to receive the gospel. The law serves this purpose for individuals and for Israel as a nation. Once we are in Jesus, the guardian is no longer needed, but until faith comes, the law serves its purpose as a guardian pressing us towards Jesus.

Those who are in Jesus are the sons of God, but if we are not yet in Jesus, we remain subject to the curses of the law. Therefore, all those

---

[9] See Genesis 32:22–32.

in Israel who are outside of Jesus remain subject to the specific curses of the Mosaic covenant, just as the Gentiles remain subject to the curses of sin as long as they are not in Jesus.

Paul addressed this issue when he spoke to a Jewish audience at the synagogue in the city of Antioch in Pisidia:

> Let it be known to you therefore, brothers, that through this man forgiveness of sins is proclaimed to you, and by him everyone who believes is freed from everything from which you could not be freed by the law of Moses. (Acts 13:38–39)

Paul's message was plain: "Everyone who believes is freed" from the curses of the law of Moses. Those who do not believe remain under the terms of the covenant, including the curses. Paul followed this promise with a sober warning from Habakkuk:

> Beware, therefore, lest what is said in the Prophets should come about: "Look, you scoffers, be astounded and perish; for I am doing a work in your days, a work that you will not believe, even if one tells it to you." (Acts 13:40–41)

The "work that you will not believe" Paul referred to was God raising up Babylon to execute His judgments against Israel. It was a statement of warning for "scoffers"—those who disobeyed God's law and did not believe the curses would result in judgment.

Paul warned the synagogue the Mosaic covenant was an ongoing threat that could only be escaped by believing in Jesus. If they did not believe in Jesus, they would become subject to the judgments of the covenant—"what is said in the prophets"—just as Israel did in Habakkuk's day.

The Transition to the New Covenant

The transition to the Mosaic covenant does not pass away immediately:

> But as it is, Christ has obtained a ministry that is as much more excellent than the old as the covenant he mediates is better, since it is enacted on better promises. . . . In speaking of a new covenant, he makes the first one obsolete. And what is becoming obsolete and growing old is ready to vanish away. (Hebrews 8:6, 13)

The Mosaic covenant is becoming obsolete, growing old, and ready to vanish away. It is obsolete because of the work of Jesus on the cross. However, it has not yet vanished. The Mosaic covenant did not pass away suddenly during Jesus' first coming. It must pass away through a process by which people subject to the covenant (Israel) call on the name of Jesus.

The Mosaic covenant is a covenant made with a single nation; therefore, for the covenant to pass away completely, the nation must be transformed in such a way that it is no longer subject to the terms of the covenant. A day must come, as Paul predicted, when all Israel:

> *will be saved, as it is written, "The Deliverer will come from Zion, he will banish ungodliness from Jacob." (Romans 11:26)*

Paul did not mean every Jewish person throughout history will be saved regardless of their relationship to Jesus. Paul was predicting a day in the future when the entire nation would be saved and forever be free of the Mosaic covenant. This is the day of salvation predicted by the prophets. It is the day when all Israel will know the Lord as Jeremiah prophesied.[10]

This is something the Mosaic covenant could never accomplish, and it is something the new covenant *must* accomplish for Israel to be free of the curses of the Mosaic covenant. *Since the new covenant depends on Jesus' righteousness and not Israel's righteousness, it is capable of creating an entirely saved nation.*

As individuals come into Jesus, the Mosaic covenant is in the process of passing away. However, a day is coming when it finally passes away, and that day requires the salvation of the same nation that made the Mosaic covenant.

This glorious salvation of all Israel is predicted numerous times in the Scripture.[11] The prophets had no idea how that day would come, but they knew it must come. For us, the mystery has now been revealed. God will bring this to pass through the redemptive work of His Son. Israel's national salvation will mean the end of the curses of the

---

[10] See Jeremiah 31:31–35.

[11] See Deuteronomy 30:1–6; Isaiah 4:3; 45:17, 25; 54:13; 59:21; 60:21; Jeremiah 31:34; 32:40; Ezekiel 20:40; 39:22, 28–29; Joel 2:26; Zechariah 12:10–14; Romans 11:26.

covenant, and so Paul referred to their salvation as "life from the dead":

> For if their rejection means the reconciliation of the world, what will their acceptance mean but life from the dead? (Romans 11:15)

Zechariah described the glory and emotions of that day when the eyes of the nation would be opened and they would be joined to Jesus as their Messiah and Savior:

> "And I will pour out on the house of David and the inhabitants of Jerusalem a spirit of grace and pleas for mercy, so that, when they look on me, on him whom they have pierced, they shall mourn for him, as one mourns for an only child, and weep bitterly over him, as one weeps over a firstborn." (Zechariah 12:10)

Throughout history, there has always been a saved remnant in Israel, and in our generation, that remnant is growing. There is a significant number of messianic believers in the land who love Jesus, and the closer we get to the end of the age, the more we will see an acceleration in the salvation of the Jewish people. We should rejoice in this and also labor for an increase. However, a saved remnant is not enough to conclude the covenant. *A day must come when all Israel is saved.*

A MODERN NATION WITH AN ANCIENT COVENANT

Nothing in history is comparable to the reemergence of Israel in 1948. It was unprecedented. Never before had a nation been restored from a people who had been scattered across the nations as a persecuted minority for nearly two thousand years. It was a statement God had not forgotten His promises for Israel, and yet her promises remain unresolved. Though modern Israel is a witness of God's mercy, Israel also lives in the midst of constant conflict. Jerusalem is trembling again, much as she did in the days of the prophets.

The nation is unable to dwell in the land in peace and safety, and is constantly harassed by various enemies. Israel faces Islamic rage, ethnic rage, and political rage. Though modern Israel is not a righteous nation, this rage is often irrational because it is not ultimately rage against Israel; it is rage against the God who chose Israel for His own purposes.

We must resist this rage. We must also expose radical groups who seek Israel's annihilation and support acts of terror to harass and destroy Israel all the while using humanitarian language to seduce the nations to rage against Israel. We cannot be complicit or silent in our generation. We must speak out against radical Islam, false justice movements, and other ideologies and movements that refuse to recognize God's covenant with Israel.

Modern Israel has deficiencies, and it is not wrong to address them. However, we must understand, agree with, and speak boldly about God's covenantal promises to her because Israel is frequently demonized and vilified in a way that is far out of proportion with her true condition.[1]

While we must resist the rage of the nations, there is more to Israel's current crisis than the rage of the nations. Biblically, any time Israel was harassed by foreign armies, God was always speaking to the nation through that harassment, and it is no different today. The modern state of Israel is under a near constant threat of foreign invasion accompanied by constant harassment by foreign armies, even armies within her borders. While we must not agree with that harassment, we must recognize the Lord is speaking to the nation through it. We must understand why the God who has regathered Israel is allowing her enemies to harass her.

A Nation Shaped by the Covenant

The Word of God is still directing and influencing international events as it did in ancient times. Modern Israel thinks her political enemies are her primary challenge, but in reality God remains Israel's main issue.

Right now, Israel is both in the land and harassed. Israel both possesses land and yet does not have her full inheritance. Modern Israel has repeatedly experienced supernatural deliverance yet still continually finds herself in an impossible situation. None of this is accidental. Israel is beloved by God yet currently an unrighteous nation at odds with Him. Because she has a unique, national covenant with Him, there are specific consequences for her sin. *The terms of the covenant are driving far more of Israel's present reality than she realizes.*

The nation's regathering demonstrates God's kind intentions towards her and His commitment to His promises. At the same time, Israel's trouble reveals the curses of the Mosaic covenant remain until the nation is saved.

When we understand the Old Testament correctly, it removes much of the mystery surrounding modern Israel and her situation. We sometimes think of God as intricately involved in the nations during ancient times but, now, mostly detached from the current geopolitical situation. In reality, God's covenants drive His interactions with the nations and, as a result, explain the current geopolitical situation.

---

[1] For more on this, see the book *One King: A Jesus Centered Answer to the Question of Zion and the People of God.*

It is important to recognize both positive and negative dimensions of the covenants can function at the same time. Israel's presence in the land and re-gathering as a nation have been completely miraculous. Over the last decades, Israel has been preserved supernaturally in military conflicts, even when the nation was totally outnumbered. Israel has technology that allows her to survive internal wars and rocket attacks with relatively limited damage. All of this is due to the kindness of God. It is a statement of His commitment to preserve Israel and bring her into her promises. However, the same harassment God defends Israel from is also a result of the negative dimensions of the covenants.

To have a full understanding of modern Israel, we have to carry both of these realities in tension. We must speak to Israel about the consequences of her sin *and* the details of her future salvation. We can see both the signs of God's discipline and the first fruits of His salvation in the rapidly growing remnant of messianic believers among the Jewish people. God is simultaneously speaking to Israel in discipline, preserving her in kindness, and moving her towards a day of salvation.

Understanding these covenantal realities does not mean we agree with evil. For example, in Habakkuk 1, God told Habakkuk he was using Babylon to speak to Israel, but that did not mean He was calling Habakkuk to overlook or agree with Babylon's sin. However, in our support for Israel, we cannot overlook the discipline of the covenant and the effect it has on the nation.

The Cry for Deliverance

Psalm 120 summarizes God's design for covenant discipline:

In my distress I called to the Lord, and he answered me. (v. 1)

Israel's pressure or "distress" is intended to cause her to call on the Lord for salvation. For this reason, the pressure of God's discipline will intensify until the nation embraces God's means of salvation. Moses summarized this in both Leviticus and Deuteronomy when he predicted God would use His discipline of Israel to break her strength:

And I will break the pride of your power, and I will make your heavens like iron and your earth like bronze. (Leviticus 26:19)

> *For the Lord will vindicate his people and have compassion on his servants, when he sees that their power is gone and there is none remaining, bond or free. (Deuteronomy 32:36)*

When the Bible predicts that God will break Israel's pride and power, it does not mean that God's objective is to destroy her. *God's objective is not to break Israel—but to break Israel's confidence in her ability to secure her promises and obtain her inheritance.* God is going to break Israel's "power" in order to get her to a Psalm 120:1 moment. Then, the nation will call on the Lord for salvation.

As we saw in the first section, Zechariah's prophecy in Zechariah 12:10–12 is a key prophecy in the New Testament. Jesus quoted it, John quoted it, and Peter alluded to it. It is prominent in New Testament descriptions of the end times because it is the day the prophets all looked forward to—the day when God's discipline results in the salvation of the entire nation and the final end of the covenant curses.

> *"And I will pour out on the house of David and the inhabitants of Jerusalem a spirit of grace and pleas for mercy, so that, when they look on me, on him whom they have pierced, they shall mourn for him, as one mourns for an only child, and weep bitterly over him, as one weeps over a firstborn." (Zechariah 12:10)*

The Nation and Her Messiah

God's discipline is one factor in Israel's trouble, but Israel also experiences the rage of Satan. The enemy knows he cannot dethrone God in the heavens, so he makes war against God in the earth by making war on God's promises. *The enemy's rage against Israel throughout Israel's history is a proxy war with the God of Israel.*

The enemy knows Israel's sin makes her vulnerable to the discipline of the covenant, and one of his end-time strategies will be to seduce Israel into sin so that her sin leaves the nation vulnerable to God's judgments. As God's judgments against Israel intensify, the enemy will take advantage of the situation and unleash his rage against Israel. The enemy will come under the delusion that God cannot deliver Israel because of her sin and the terms of His covenant with her.

What happened to Jesus is a picture of what will happen to Israel at the end of the age. When Jesus entered into His suffering, the enemy saw God put the guilt of our sin on Jesus.[2] The "rulers of this age" (a reference to spiritual powers) participated in Jesus' crucifixion because they did not understand what was happening. They saw Jesus' judgment as an opportunity to release their rage against Him.

> *None of the rulers of this age understood this, for if they had, they would not have crucified the Lord of glory. (1 Corinthians 2:8)*

The rulers could not see a way the Father could save Jesus because their rage blinded them to the mystery of redemption. Because they do not understand mercy, they eagerly crucified Jesus. However, the crucified Jesus suddenly became the resurrected Jesus. They thought they had defeated Jesus, but the event they thought was their greatest victory set the stage for their greatest defeat.[3]

Paul described Jesus' death and resurrection as the wisdom of God that the rulers did not understand:

> *For the word of the cross is folly to those who are perishing, but to us who are being saved it is the power of God. For it is written, "I will destroy the wisdom of the wise, and the discernment of the discerning I will thwart." (1 Corinthians 1:18–19)*

First Corinthians 1:18 is a quote of Isaiah 29:14:

> *"Therefore, behold, I will again do wonderful things with this people, with wonder upon wonder; and the wisdom of their wise men shall perish, and the discernment of their discerning men shall be hidden."*

In Isaiah 29, God predicted what He would do with "this people," referring to Israel. It's a very dramatic prophecy. It describes a siege on Jerusalem that seeks to bring Israel "down to the dust," meaning to destroy her.

> *Ah, Ariel, Ariel, the city where David encamped! Add year to year; let the feasts run their round. Yet I will distress Ariel, and there shall be moaning and lamentation, and she shall be to me like an Ariel. And I will encamp against you all around, and will besiege you with towers and I will raise siegeworks against you. And you will be brought low; from the*

---

[2] See 1 Peter 2:24.

[3] See Romans 1:4; 1 Corinthians 15:24–26; 2 Timothy 1:10; Hebrews 2:14.

earth you shall speak, and from the dust your speech will be bowed down;
your voice shall come from the ground like the voice of a ghost, and from
the dust your speech shall whisper. (Isaiah 29:1–4)

God described His own involvement in the siege in verses 2 and 3. However, in the middle of the siege, something unexpected happens. Israel's enemies are so profoundly defeated that the entire siege seems like a dream:

But the multitude of your foreign foes shall be like small dust, and the
multitude of the ruthless like passing chaff. And in an instant, suddenly,
you will be visited by the Lord of hosts with thunder and with earthquake
and great noise, with whirlwind and tempest, and the flame of a
devouring fire. And the multitude of all the nations that fight against
Ariel, all that fight against her and her stronghold and distress her, shall
be like a dream, a vision of the night. (Isaiah 29:5–7)

Isaiah 29 prophesies a day when God allows Israel's enemies to come against her. Her enemies will seize the opportunity in a rage, believing they can destroy God's promises and prevent His judgments. However, this moment of intense pressure will cause Israel to cry out to her God, and God will deliver her suddenly and shockingly.[4] Paul connected Isaiah 29 with 1 Corinthians 1 because Jesus was a prophetic picture of how the wisdom of God would be displayed in Israel's salvation.

A day is coming when Israel will be vulnerable to the judgments of God because of her sin and the covenants. In that moment, her enemies will rage and try to take advantage of Israel's discipline by laying siege on Jerusalem. However, God will use the situation to cause Israel to cry out for salvation.

When Israel's condition seems to be hopeless, God will suddenly save her from the vengeance of her enemies and, instead, release His vengeance on the nations and on the one who sought to destroy Israel in her moment of compromise, weakness, and vulnerability.[5] God's supernatural deliverance of His Son is a picture of His final deliverance

----

[4] See Isaiah 34; Joel 3; Zechariah 12–14.

[5] See Isaiah 14:19; Daniel 7:11; Revelation 19:20.

of Israel. Jesus is so closely bound to Israel that there is a sense in which He lived out Israel's story.

Israel is unsaved, and the nations are called to tenderly but boldly call her to repentance. However, Israel remains called, and God remains committed to Israel in the same way a father remains committed to a child—even when that child is disobedient. Because they cannot grasp mercy, the rulers and nations are blind to the certainty of God's plan, but Israel's entrance into her own destiny is just as assured as Jesus' entry into His destiny.

Israel's Story Is Our Story

We are called to recognize God's dealings with Israel so we can affirm Israel's covenantal destiny and speak prophetically to her about what God requires of her to enter into that destiny.

When we understand God's relationship with Israel, we better understand His relationship with us. God's law requires Israel to be righteous, but ultimately God requires all men to be righteous. God's law brings judgment on Israel, but His law will bring judgment on all men in the end. Both Israel and the nations experience God's mercy and kindness even when they are subject to judgment.

What God is doing with Israel is the same thing He does with every believer. He brings us to the point where we no longer have any confidence in our ability so that we will turn to Him for salvation. Paul expressed this in Philippians 3:3:

> *For we are the circumcision, who worship by the Spirit of God and glory in Christ Jesus and put no confidence in the flesh.*

God's just requirements of Israel and the nations serve as a glorious tutor to bring us to Jesus. The law is not only going to bring individuals to salvation, it is going to bring an entire nation to Jesus.

Part 4: God's Promise to the Nations

GOD ALWAYS HAD THE NATIONS IN MIND

Because of Israel's unique place in God's story, a significant amount of the end-time drama revolves around God resolving Israel's situation and fulfilling Israel's promises. However, Israel's story is part of God's story for the nations. *God began His plan with Abraham out of His desire to save the nations.* Therefore, we must also understand God's promise to the nations, how the Bible describes the fulfillment of that promise, and how it also sets the stage for end-time events.

When God began the redemptive plan with Abraham, He intended to bring salvation to the nations:

> *And the Scripture, foreseeing that God would justify the Gentiles by faith, preached the gospel beforehand to Abraham, saying, "In you shall all the nations be blessed."[1] (Galatians 3:8)*

The nations were not an afterthought to God, and the salvation of the Gentiles was not a new idea because Israel had failed in her covenant calling. God made covenant with Abraham in order to save the nations. The New Testament is not the end of Israel's story, but it is also not the beginning of the story of the nations. Paul reminded the church in Ephesus—composed primarily of Gentiles—God had them in His mind before the foundation of the world:

> *Blessed be the God and Father of our Lord Jesus Christ, who has blessed us in Christ with every spiritual blessing in the heavenly places, even as he chose us in him before the foundation of the world, that we should be holy and blameless before him. In love he predestined us for adoption to himself as sons through Jesus Christ, according to the purpose of his will. (Ephesians 1:3–5)*

---

[1] See Genesis 12:3.

124 IT MUST BE FINISHED

The verses describing the end-time church help us understand God's purposes for the nations and what must happen before the return of Jesus.

Abraham's Three Promises Are Tightly Woven Together

As redemptive history unfolds, all three promises also become interdependent. The nations cannot receive the knowledge of God and salvation apart from God's work through Israel.[2] At the same time, Israel's salvation depends on a witness that will come from the nations.[3] God has made us *all* interdependent so that we *all* embrace humility.

Jesus came to confirm—we could also say "guarantee"—the promises made to the Jewish patriarchs so that the Gentiles would glorify God for His mercy:

> *For I tell you that Christ became a servant to the circumcised to show God's truthfulness, in order to confirm the promises given to the patriarchs, and in order that the Gentiles might glorify God for his mercy. As it is written, "Therefore I will praise you among the Gentiles, and sing to your name." (Romans 15:8–9)*

God's promises to Israel and the nations are so intimately connected the redemptive plan unites Jew and Gentile into one body. Paul referred to God's plan to bring together Jew and Gentile as the *mystery of Christ*:

> *Remember that you were at that time separate from Christ, excluded from the commonwealth of Israel, and strangers to the covenants of promise, having no hope and without God in the world. But now in Christ Jesus you who formerly were far off have been brought near by the blood of Christ. For He Himself is our peace, who made both groups into one and broke down the barrier of the dividing wall, by abolishing in His flesh the enmity, which is the Law of commandments contained in ordinances, so that in Himself He might make the two into one new man, thus establishing peace, and might reconcile them both in one body to God through the cross, by it having put to death the enmity. (Ephesians 2:12–16 NASB)*

---

[2] See Romans 9:4–5.

[3] See Romans 10:19–21; 11:11–12, 25–26.

That by revelation there was made known to me the mystery, as I wrote before in brief. By referring to this, when you read you can understand my insight into the mystery of Christ, which in other generations was not made known to the sons of men, as it has now been revealed to His holy apostles and prophets in the Spirit; to be specific, that the Gentiles are fellow heirs and fellow members of the body, and fellow partakers of the promise in Christ Jesus through the gospel. (3:3–6 NASB)

God's plan to fulfill Abraham's promises includes distinct promises to Israel, but also involves bringing Jew and Gentile together in one body. Because Israel and the Gentiles are one family in Jesus, it means we will receive the promises made to us together, as a family, at the same time.

God's Desire for the Nations

While no one knew just how God would save the nations, from the beginning the Bible promised God would have a people in Israel and the nations. Because the promises in the Old and New Testament are fulfilled in the context of the church, these promises reveal both God's plan for Israel and His plan for the nations. *Therefore, predictions the prophets made of a people in the nations worshipping the God of Israel are descriptions of the mature, end-time church.* Studying these predictions gives us a picture of what the fulfillment of Abraham's third promise looks like.

When you read the Old Testament, you can feel God's desire for the nations:

"As for me, I have set my King on Zion, my holy hill." I will tell of the decree: The Lord said to me, "You are my Son; today I have begotten you. Ask of me, and I will make the nations your heritage, and the ends of the earth your possession." (Psalm 2:6–8)

May God be gracious to us and bless us and make his face to shine upon us, Selah that your way may be known on earth, your saving power among all nations. Let the peoples praise you, O God; let all the peoples praise you! Let the nations be glad and sing for joy, for you judge the peoples with equity and guide the nations upon earth. Selah let the peoples praise you, O God; let all the peoples praise you! (67:1–5)

All the nations you have made shall come and worship before you, O Lord, and shall glorify your name. (86:9)

Oh sing to the Lord a new song; sing to the Lord, all the earth! Sing to the Lord, bless his name; tell of his salvation from day to day. Declare his glory among the nations, his marvelous works among all the peoples! (96:1–3)

They lift up their voices, they sing for joy; over the majesty of the Lord they shout from the west. Therefore in the east give glory to the Lord; in the coastlands of the sea, give glory to the name of the Lord, the God of Israel. From the ends of the earth we hear songs of praise, of glory to the Righteous One. (Isaiah 24:14–16)

Behold my servant, whom I uphold, my chosen, in whom my soul delights; I have put my Spirit upon him; he will bring forth justice to the nations. (42:1)

"I am the Lord; I have called you in righteousness; I will take you by the hand and keep you; I will give you as a covenant for the people, a light for the nations." (42:6)

"Turn to me and be saved, all the ends of the earth! For I am God, and there is no other." (45:22)

He says: "It is too light a thing that you should be my servant to raise up the tribes of Jacob and to bring back the preserved of Israel; I will make you as a light for the nations, that my salvation may reach to the end of the earth." (49:6)

Sing and rejoice, O daughter of Zion, for behold, I come and I will dwell in your midst, declares the Lord. And many nations shall join themselves to the Lord in that day, and shall be my people. And I will dwell in your midst, and you shall know that the Lord of hosts has sent me to you. (Zechariah 2:10–11)

For from the rising of the sun to its setting my name will be great among the nations, and in every place incense will be offered to my name, and a pure offering. For my name will be great among the nations, says the Lord of hosts. (Malachi 1:11)

The book of Jonah is an example of God's deep desire for the nations. God sent Jonah to preach to a wicked nation that was Israel's enemy, and Jonah was intensely frustrated because he knew God wanted to show Assyria mercy:

> *O Lord, is not this what I said when I was yet in my country? That is why I made haste to flee to Tarshish; for I knew that you are a gracious God and merciful, slow to anger and abounding in steadfast love, and relenting from disaster. (Jonah 4:2)*

God's final statement to Jonah reveals God's great heart for the Gentiles—even the ones considered most wicked:

> *And the Lord said, "You pity the plant, for which you did not labor, nor did you make it grow, which came into being in a night and perished in a night. And should not I pity Nineveh, that great city, in which there are more than 120,000 persons who do not know their right hand from their left, and also much cattle?" (Jonah 4:10–11)*

While the Old Testament focuses primarily on Israel's story, it also makes it clear that God has the nations in mind. This becomes even clearer in the New Testament.

Each time Jesus commissioned the disciples, He sent them to the nations:

> *"And this gospel of the kingdom will be proclaimed throughout the whole world as a testimony to all nations, and then the end will come." (Matthew 24:14)*

> *"Go therefore and make disciples of all nations, baptizing them in the name of the Father and of the Son and of the Holy Spirit." (28:19)*

> *"But you will receive power when the Holy Spirit has come upon you, and you will be my witnesses in Jerusalem and in all Judea and Samaria, and to the end of the earth." (Acts 1:8)*

Paul described God's great plan to save the Gentiles and bring them to fullness:

> *Or is God the God of Jews only? Is he not the God of Gentiles also? Yes, of Gentiles also, since God is one—who will justify the circumcised by faith and the uncircumcised through faith. (Romans 3:29–30)*

Lest you be wise in your own sight, I do not want you to be unaware of this mystery, brothers: a partial hardening has come upon Israel, until the fullness of the Gentiles has come in. (11:25)

For I tell you that Christ became a servant to the circumcised to show God's truthfulness, in order to confirm the promises given to the patriarchs, and in order that the Gentiles might glorify God for his mercy. As it is written, "Therefore I will praise you among the Gentiles, and sing to your name." And again it is said, "Rejoice, O Gentiles, with his people." And again, "Praise the Lord, all you Gentiles, and let all the peoples extol him." And again Isaiah says, "The root of Jesse will come, even he who arises to rule the Gentiles; in him will the Gentiles hope." (15:8–12)

The Church—A Witness of Another Kingdom

Paul described the church as God's "ambassadors" because our citizenship is in heaven.[4] Paul's analogy of the church as a people of ambassadors is one of the best ways to understand the kingdom of God in this age.

Each church in the nations is an embassy of another kingdom. We live in the kingdoms of this world, but we represent another kingdom. In the same way that a country's embassy is not the fullness of that country but a representation of it, so also the church in this age is not the fullness of the kingdom, but it points to the kingdom that is coming.

The church in this age is not the fullness of the kingdom, but each church is a valid expression of the kingdom. When people come into the church, they experience the values and the power of the kingdom the church points to. Our assignment in this age is to build as many "embassies" of the coming kingdom as we can.

The church is a place in this age where people can taste the kingdom that is coming. It is God's provision for the nations during the end times. Through the church, the nations will experience the power of the coming kingdom, be invited to resist the Antichrist, and declare loyalty to the coming King.

---

[4] See 2 Corinthians 5:20; Ephesians 6:20; Philippians 3:20.

The End-Time Church Will Be a Mature Church

Paul predicted God's activity in the nations would produce a mature church:

> *And he gave the apostles, the prophets, the evangelists, the shepherds and teachers, to equip the saints for the work of ministry, for building up the body of Christ, until we all attain to the unity of the faith and of the knowledge of the Son of God, to mature manhood, to the measure of the stature of the fullness of Christ. (Ephesians 4:11–13)*

Paul's prediction is profound: The church will come to the knowledge of God, mature manhood, and the measure of the stature of the fullness of Christ. This is what must be accomplished in her before Jesus returns. It is the reason Jesus died:

> *Husbands, love your wives, as Christ loved the church and gave himself up for her, that he might sanctify her, having cleansed her by the washing of water with the word, so that he might present the church to himself in splendor, without spot or wrinkle or any such thing, that she might be holy and without blemish. (Ephesians 5:25–27)*

Paul identified several things Jesus' suffering will accomplish for the church. It sanctifies the church. The word *sanctifies* means *set apart for a special purpose* and includes the idea of holiness. It cleanses the church. In the same way that ancient Israelites washed themselves ceremonially in order to approach God, Jesus' words cleanse the church. Jesus is committed to presenting a church clothed in splendor without spot, wrinkle, or any kind of imperfection.

Paul used the analogy of marriage to describe Jesus' relationship to the church. Jesus will bring the church to maturity because He died in order to have a church that is holy and without blemish. John the Baptist used this same analogy when he described Jesus as a Bridegroom and used a wedding analogy to describe his ministry of preparing the people for Jesus:

> *The one who has the bride is the bridegroom. The friend of the bridegroom, who stands and hears him, rejoices greatly at the bridegroom's voice. Therefore this joy of mine is now complete. (John 3:29)*

When we think of a bride and a wedding, we think of a mature and beautiful woman who has taken every effort to be attractive to her bridegroom. The same is true of the church. Jesus died so the church can be mature and beautiful—a partner fit for Him. As a result, the marriage analogy is used throughout the New Testament to describe the final condition of the church:

Even as he chose us in him before the foundation of the world, that we should be holy and blameless before him. In love. . . . (Ephesians 1:4)

For I feel a divine jealousy for you, since I betrothed you to one husband, to present you as a pure virgin to Christ. (2 Corinthians 11:2)

He has now reconciled in his body of flesh by his death, in order to present you holy and blameless and above reproach before him. (Colossians 1:22)

Him we proclaim, warning everyone and teaching everyone with all wisdom, that we may present everyone mature in Christ. (1:28)

"Let us rejoice and exult and give him the glory, for the marriage of the Lamb has come, and his Bride has made herself ready; it was granted her to clothe herself with fine linen, bright and pure"—for the fine linen is the righteous deeds of the saints. And the angel said to me, "Write this: Blessed are those who are invited to the marriage supper of the Lamb." And he said to me, "These are the true words of God." (Revelation 19:7–9)

The Father wants to give His Son a bride from the nations as a reward for His suffering. For that reason, the Father will mature the church until she becomes a beautiful bride for His Son. The end of the age is the time when the church comes to maturity and is ready to be joined with Jesus forever. And so, the Bible compares Jesus' return to a great wedding celebration.

It is not an accident that Jesus performed His first miracle at a wedding, and the people's response to the miracle is a prophetic statement for us. God's best things are to come:

"Everyone serves the good wine first, and when people have drunk freely, then the poor wine. But you have kept the good wine until now." (John 2:10)

Jesus is not returning for a bride who is barely surviving; He is returning for a mature church the powers of hell cannot overcome:

> *"And I tell you, you are Peter, and on this rock I will build my church, and the gates of hell shall not prevail against it." (Matthew 16:18)*

All of this is part of what it means for the nations to be blessed. We have greatly underestimated the glory that God is going to put on the church. The Bible even promises when we see Jesus we will be like Him.

> *Who will transform our lowly body to be like his glorious body, by the power that enables him even to subject all things to himself. (Philippians 3:21)*

> *It was for this He called you through our gospel, that you may gain the glory of our Lord Jesus Christ. (2 Thessalonians 2:14 NASB)*

> *Beloved, we are God's children now, and what we will be has not yet appeared; but we know that when he appears we shall be like him, because we shall see him as he is. (1 John 3:2)*

No matter what immaturity we may see in the church now, the Bible promises a mature church will emerge. The church is going to become so glorious she will be clothed with a glory similar to Jesus' own glory and become a suitable partner for Him for all eternity. The church consists of both Jew and Gentile, so this is a promise for all people groups, but it has profound implications for the church in the nations.

The Old Testament predicted that a day would come when all Israel would be saved and the nations would be blessed, but the New Testament brings greater focus to that promise. Israel will be saved as a nation, but a saved remnant must also come from every people group for the age to end.[5] This people—both Jew and Gentile—will be mature at Jesus' return.

The end-time church will be deeply loyal to Jesus and live with great anticipation of His return.

---

[5] See Revelation 5:9; 7:9.

And they overcame him because of the blood of the Lamb and because of the word of their testimony, and they did not love their life even when faced with death. (Revelation 12:11 NASB)

And I saw something like a sea of glass mixed with fire, and those who had been victorious over the beast and his image and the number of his name, standing on the sea of glass, holding harps of God. And they sang the song of Moses, the bond-servant of God, and the song of the Lamb, saying, "Great and marvelous are Your works, O Lord God, the Almighty; Righteous and true are Your ways, King of the nations! "Who will not fear, O Lord, and glorify Your name? For You alone are holy; for ALL THE NATIONS WILL COME AND WORSHIP BEFORE YOU, FOR YOUR RIGHTEOUS ACTS HAVE BEEN REVEALED." (Revelation 15:2–4 NASB)

Daniel also described the maturity of the end-time church:

He shall seduce with flattery those who violate the covenant, but the people who know their God shall stand firm and take action. And the wise among the people shall make many understand, though for some days they shall stumble by sword and flame, by captivity and plunder. (Daniel 11:32–33)

And those who are wise shall shine like the brightness of the sky above; and those who turn many to righteousness, like the stars forever and ever. (12:3)

The end-time church will be a people who know their God, stand firm in the face of the Antichrist, and "take action." They will instruct many people and cause them to also understand the Word of God. They will "turn many to righteousness." Though the end-time church will be persecuted by the Antichrist, Daniel was told the end-time church will be missional, mature, and influence many to turn to righteousness.

When we summarize what the Bible says about the end-time church, it gives us a vivid picture of what God is going to do in the nations. The end-time church will be like a mature bride. She will be deeply in love with Jesus, worshipping God for all His mighty deeds, even in the middle of great tribulation. She will be faithful and loyal to Jesus, even unto death. She will be an active influence in the earth, continuing to call others to righteousness. This prediction is not limited to just one part of the body. We are told this will be the condition of the church in every people group before the Lord returns:

> *After these things I looked, and behold, a great multitude which no one could count, from every nation and all tribes and peoples and tongues, standing before the throne and before the Lamb, clothed in white robes, and palm branches were in their hands. . . . These are the ones who come out of the great tribulation, and they have washed their robes and made them white in the blood of the Lamb. (Revelation 7:9, 14 NASB)*

None of these predictions minimize the great trials, persecution, suffering, conflicts, and tests the end-time church will face. The Bible predicts many end-time saints will lose their lives because of their faithfulness to Jesus. However, suffering and faithfulness unto death are not signs of a weak church. They are the indicators of a strong, vibrant, and mature church able to withstand the most wicked ruler in history.

The Church Will Mature in Glory and Crisis

We can hardly anticipate all that was in God's heart and mind when he gave Abraham the promise to bless the nations in Genesis 12:3. That blessing is described throughout history, and it will come to pass before the age ends. *Just as we can hardly anticipate the glory of Israel's salvation, so we can hardly anticipate the glory that is coming on the mature church.*

The end times are a time of glory as the church comes to maturity and also a time of unparalleled crisis when the Antichrist takes the stage of human history. To have an accurate picture of the end times, we cannot underestimate either one of these themes.

Some have underestimated the glory of the mature, end-time church. When we do this, we miss what the Bible says about the church, the Antichrist dominates our thinking, and we become driven by fear with no faith for what God will do in the middle of the end times. This explains why we have examined what the Bible says about the end-time church.

Others focus only on the church and do not soberly consider what the Bible says about the end-time crisis. It will be an unparalleled time of trouble. When we think of the massive crises throughout history, none of them come close. This one will exceed them all. The prophets

134 It Must Be Finished

used dramatic language to describe what will happen so that we will be prepared for it. We cannot ignore or minimize what the Bible says:

They will be dismayed: pangs and agony will seize them; they will be in anguish like a woman in labor. They will look aghast at one another; their faces will be aflame. (Isaiah 13:8)

For this reason my loins are full of anguish; pains have seized me like the pains of a woman in labor. I am so bewildered I cannot hear, so terrified I cannot see. (Isaiah 21:3 NASB)

Ask now, and see, can a man bear a child? Why then do I see every man with his hands on his stomach like a woman in labor? Why has every face turned pale? Alas! That day is so great there is none like it; it is a time of distress for Jacob; yet he shall be saved out of it. (Jeremiah 30:6–7)

"At that time shall arise Michael, the great prince who has charge of your people. And there shall be a time of trouble, such as never has been since there was a nation till that time. But at that time your people shall be delivered, everyone whose name shall be found written in the book." (Daniel 12:1)

Alas, you who are longing for the day of the Lord, for what purpose will the day of the Lord be to you? It will be darkness and not light. (Amos 5:18 NASB)

A day of wrath is that day, a day of trouble and distress, a day of destruction and desolation, a day of darkness and gloom, a day of clouds and thick darkness, a day of trumpet and battle cry against the fortified cities and the high corner towers. (Zephaniah 1:15–16 NASB)

"For then there will be a great tribulation, such as has not occurred since the beginning of the world until now, nor ever will." (Matthew 24:21 NASB)

"Therefore, rejoice, O heavens and you who dwell in them! But woe to you, O earth and sea, for the devil has come down to you in great wrath, because he knows that his time is short!" (Revelation 12:12)

We cannot soften the blows of these verses. Something is coming that goes beyond every crisis history has experienced up to this point.

It will be the final conflict between God and His enemies for the salvation and restoration of the earth.

However, in the middle of this crisis, God will have a people. They will be mature and unoffended. They will know their God, have understanding about the end-time crisis, stand firm, and take action.

The end times will be unprecedented in their trouble, but simultaneously, they will be a time of missions. The church will not only be resisting the enemy's activity; the church will be active in God's work. *The gospel will expand even during the reign of the Antichrist.*

A GREAT END-TIME HARVEST IN THE NATIONS

God's promise to the nations will be fulfilled by a great harvest that will impact every people group. *The salvation of the nations, like Israel's national salvation, is a key event associated with the return of the Lord and predicted throughout the book of Revelation:*

> *And they sang a new song, saying, "Worthy are you to take the scroll and to open its seals, for you were slain, and by your blood you ransomed people for God from every tribe and language and people and nation." (5:9)*

> *After this I looked, and behold, a great multitude that no one could number, from every nation, from all tribes and peoples and languages, standing before the throne and before the Lamb, clothed in white robes, with palm branches in their hands. (7:9)*

> *Then I saw another angel flying directly overhead, with an eternal gospel to proclaim to those who dwell on earth, to every nation and tribe and language and people. (14:6)*

> *"Who will not fear, O Lord, and glorify your name? For you alone are holy. All nations will come and worship you, for your righteous acts have been revealed." (15:4)*

These verses are evidence of a great harvest in the nations before Jesus returns. They reveal the gospel will be preached through the nations all the way to the return of Jesus—even during the end times. This means missions will be ongoing even during the reign of the Antichrist.

The Scope of the End-Time Harvest

The Scripture repeatedly predicts a harvest in the nations, but the book of Revelation is the only book that shows us the results of that harvest because the final harvest will come during the end times.[1] Revelation 7 describes the scope of the end-time revival that is part of God's promise to the nations:

> *After this I looked, and behold, a great multitude that no one could number, from every nation, from all tribes and peoples and languages, standing before the throne and before the Lamb, clothed in white robes, with palm branches in their hands, and crying out with a loud voice, "Salvation belongs to our God who sits on the throne, and to the Lamb!" . . . Then one of the elders addressed me, saying, "Who are these, clothed in white robes, and from where have they come?" I said to him, "Sir, you know." And he said to me, "These are the ones coming out of the great tribulation. They have washed their robes and made them white in the blood of the Lamb. (vv. 9–10, 13–14)*

The elder asked John one question—"Who are these people, and where do they come from?"—to communicate to John that the timing of the fulfillment of this vision was important. This is what the church will look like in the final generation, and the details of the vision were given so we can understand the condition of the end-time church. Most commentators believe these are the martyrs of the great tribulation, but regardless of whether John saw only the martyrs of the great tribulation or the entire end-time church, the message is profound.

John saw a massive number of people—a multitude that could not be numbered. Many people tend to assume the end-time church will barely survive, but John saw something completely different. We cannot know exactly how large the end-time church will be or what percentage of the earth's population it will include, but it clearly will be substantial. As a point of comparison, in Revelation 9:16, John described an army of two hundred million, so the fact that no one can number this multitude means it is an incredibly large group of people.

Not only did John see an enormous church, he also saw a church which came from every tribe and tongue. This means there will be a

---

[1] See Revelation 5:9; 7:9.

mature church in every people group. When God fulfills His promise to the nations, every single people group or nation will be represented.

Something tremendous must happen to produce the multitude John saw. This kind of church must be the result of a great harvest beyond anything we have seen in history. This is a prediction that great revival will sweep the earth, touch every people group, and result in a significant harvest in the nations.

We are also told this revival will be so profound it will result in some of Israel's greatest enemies becoming fully devoted to Jesus and partnering with His purposes. For example, Isaiah 19 predicts a dramatic transformation in nations that have historically been Israel's enemies:

> *In that day Israel will be the third with Egypt and Assyria, a blessing in the midst of the earth, whom the Lord of hosts has blessed, saying, "Blessed be Egypt my people, and Assyria the work of my hands, and Israel my inheritance." (vv. 24–25)*

The fact that this harvest will happen during the rule of the Antichrist is astounding.

Harvest language is all throughout the New Testament. Recognizing this language and how the New Testament authors used it is key to understanding the Bible's prediction of a great end-time harvest.

John the Baptist described Jesus as the One who would harvest the earth:[2]

> *His winnowing fork is in his hand, and he will clear his threshing floor and gather his wheat into the barn, but the chaff he will burn with unquenchable fire. (Matthew 3:12)*

Jesus described His second coming as the time of harvest:[3]

> *He put another parable before them, saying, "The kingdom of heaven may be compared to a man who sowed good seed in his field, but while his men were sleeping, his enemy came and sowed weeds among the wheat and went away. So when the plants came up and bore grain, then the weeds appeared also. And the servants of the master of the house came and*

---

[2] See also Luke 3:17.

[3] See also Mark 4:26–29.

said to him, 'Master, did you not sow good seed in your field? How then does it have weeds?' He said to them, 'An enemy has done this.' So the servants said to him, 'Then do you want us to go and gather them?' But he said, 'No, lest in gathering the weeds you root up the wheat along with them. Let both grow together until the harvest, and at harvest time I will tell the reapers, "Gather the weeds first and bind them in bundles to be burned, but gather the wheat into my barn."'' (Matthew 13:24–30)

Jesus also used a fishing analogy to describe the end of the age. He described the end of the age as the time when the nets would be full and the fish of the "harvest" would be caught—both good and evil:

Again, the kingdom of heaven is like a net that was thrown into the sea and gathered fish of every kind. When it was full, men drew it ashore and sat down and sorted the good into containers but threw away the bad. So it will be at the end of the age. (Matthew 13:47–49)

The book of Revelation also contains the same harvest language:

Then I looked, and behold, a white cloud, and sitting on the cloud was one like a son of man, having a golden crown on His head and a sharp sickle in His hand. And another angel came out of the temple, crying out with a loud voice to Him who sat on the cloud, "Put in your sickle and reap, for the hour to reap has come, because the harvest of the earth is ripe." Then He who sat on the cloud swung His sickle over the earth, and the earth was reaped. And another angel came out of the temple which is in heaven, and he also had a sharp sickle. Then another angel, the one who has power over fire, came out from the altar; and he called with a loud voice to him who had the sharp sickle, saying, "Put in your sharp sickle and gather the clusters from the vine of the earth, because her grapes are ripe." So the angel swung his sickle to the earth and gathered the clusters from the vine of the earth, and threw them into the great wine press of the wrath of God. And the wine press was trodden outside the city, and blood came out from the wine press, up to the horses' bridles, for a distance of two hundred miles. (14:14–20 NASB)

In these analogies, the end of the age is the great harvest for *both* righteousness and wickedness. When we neglect either harvest, we end up with an incomplete view of the end times. The church will come to fullness and evil will reach its climax in the same generation. This will make the end of the age a spectacular time, unlike any other time in history.

Israel's Agricultural Cycle—A Prediction of End-Time Harvest

When the authors of the Bible used the language of harvest, they had ancient Israel's agricultural cycle in mind. Becoming familiar with this cycle helps us understand why they expected a great end-time harvest. This cycle began in the fall with what were called *the early rains.* These rains ended the dryness of summer and produced a harvest of things like nuts and tree fruits. The early harvest sustained the people, and the early rains softened the ground so it could be worked to produce a later harvest. After the early rains, farmers would work the ground and prepare for a second set of rains and a second time of harvest.

In the spring, this second set of rains—called *the late⁴ rains*—would come. They were much heavier than the early rains, and they were critical because they prepared Israel's main crops for harvest. This was the time when the primary staples like wheat and barley were harvested.

The two rains and two harvests were connected. Without the early rains, there was no food to sustain the people, and the ground was not prepared for the subsequent work. Without the early rains, the later rains would fall on hard, dry ground and destroy everything. The later rains depended on the early rains, but the later rains were much heavier and brought a much larger harvest. This larger harvest marked the end of the growing season.

The biblical phrase *firstfruits* is used to refer to the first part of the harvest after the early rains. Paul used that metaphor to describe the present gift of the Spirit we enjoy compared to what we will enjoy when we are resurrected from the dead and receive all the benefits of our salvation. Paul described what we currently have as the *firstfruits* or *early harvest,* and he expected the greater *late harvest* to come at the resurrection, which comes at the return of the Lord.[5]

---

⁴ This is where we get the term *latter rain.*

⁵ See 1 Corinthians 15:23; 1 Thessalonians 4:16–18.

And not only the creation, but we ourselves, who have the firstfruits of the
Spirit, groan inwardly as we wait eagerly for adoption as sons, the
redemption of our bodies. (Romans 8:23)

The apostles used Israel's cycle of harvest to describe what God
was doing in their generation, and this reveals their expectation for a
future great harvest that would occur at the end of the age when the
church came into maturity. For example, Paul and James both referred
to the early church as a *firstfruits* of the harvest that was coming:

But we ought always to give thanks to God for you, brothers beloved by
the Lord, because God chose you as the firstfruits to be saved, through
sanctification by the Spirit and belief in the truth. (2 Thessalonians
2:13)

Of his own will he brought us forth by the word of truth, that we should
be a kind of firstfruits of his creatures. (James 1:18)

The early church understood that the rain of the Spirit in their generation was an "early rain" that had produced an "early harvest" (or
first fruits) and that a later rain would come to bring in a later (and
larger) harvest. The idea of an early harvest without a second, greater
harvest or an early rain without a harder, heavier later rain would have
been very confusing to the first-century church.

Their understanding of God's plan was fairly simple: The outpouring of the Spirit in Acts 2 was an early rain to soften the ground and
enable the church to labor. However, that rain was not the final rain.
The labor of the church was to prepare the nations for a coming great
rain that would result in the great harvest of the earth which would
come at the end of the age.

The Apostles' Expectation of Harvest

It is critical to understand Israel's harvest cycle to properly interpret
what the apostles believed about the end of the age. This cycle of harvest is the key that unlocks the book of Acts, and it has implications
for the end-time move of God.

Peter's perspective of harvest was what caused him to describe the
outpouring of the Spirit as a manifestation of Joel's prophecy:

But this is what was uttered through the prophet Joel: "'And in the last days it shall be, God declares, that I will pour out my Spirit on all flesh, and your sons and your daughters shall prophesy, and your young men shall see visions, and your old men shall dream dreams.'" (Acts 2:16–17)

Joel predicted an outpouring of the Spirit accompanied by the deliverance of Israel and dramatic end-time signs in the earth. None of these things happened in Peter's generation, and yet Peter clearly saw a connection between Acts 2 and Joel's prophecy because of Joel 2:23:

"Be glad, O children of Zion, and rejoice in the Lord your God, for he has given the early rain for your vindication; he has poured down for you abundant rain, the early and the latter rain, as before."

In Joel 2:23, the prophet reminded his readers that the Lord gave abundant rain in the form of early and later rains with accompanying early and later harvests. Peter recognized what was happening in Acts 2 as an early rain and early harvest of what was to come. What happened in the book of Acts was directly connected to the fulfillment of Joel's prophecy because it began with an outpouring of the Spirit and resulted in a harvest both in Israel and among the Gentiles.

However, the events in Acts clearly were not the fulfillment of all that Joel prophesied. As Joel prophesied, there must be an early rain and then a later rain. The key to understanding how Peter connected the day of Pentecost with Joel's prophecy is realizing Peter understood Pentecost as an early rain that pointed to a much harder, later rain.

The book of Joel and the book of Acts interpret each other. The book of Joel speaks of the early rains but focuses primarily on the end-time outpouring of the Spirit and God's end-time judgments. The book of Acts is the opposite. It speaks of the end-time outpouring and end-time judgments but focuses primarily on the early rains and early harvest of the church.

In the same way early rains produce a smaller harvest and prepare the ground to receive the later rain, so also the work that God began in the book of Acts has produced a harvest in the nations and prepared them to receive the harder, later rains. However, God's harvest in the nations is incomplete until a final rain that is much greater in scope than Acts 2 falls and produces a much greater harvest than what the first-century church experienced.

Using the agricultural calendar of Israel as an analogy, Gods' work in the Old Testament was like Israel's dry summer. That dry summer ended with the early rains of the Spirit which produced an initial harvest. This is what began on the day of Pentecost. It inaugurated a season of planting and harvesting (Peter referred to this as the broader *last days*), leading to a time when God would release the great later rains which bring the later, and bigger, harvest to maturity.

James used this analogy of early and later rains, and early and later harvests, to summarize God's work in the time between Jesus' first and second coming:

> *Be patient, therefore, brothers, until the coming of the Lord. See how the farmer waits for the precious fruit of the earth, being patient about it, until it receives the early and the late rains. (James 5:7)*

We live after the early rain but before the late rain, and we are called to labor in the nations to prepare for the late rain and the great harvest. The book of Acts describes the early rain and harvest and so provides a picture of what the final harvest will look like. The book of Acts describes a regional outpouring of the Spirit, but the end-time outpouring of the Spirit is global. Acts describes a regional harvest among Jews and Gentiles in the Roman Empire, but the end-time revival produces a global harvest from every tribe and tongue.

Acts is a pattern we can use to understand what the Bible predicts about the end-time revival. The early rains on the day of Pentecost did not fulfill Joel's prophecy, but they are part of Joel's prophecy that said an early rain would come. Acts 2 is a small picture of the coming outpouring of the Spirit that will fulfill Joel 2.

The outpouring of the Spirit on the day of Pentecost was a guarantee the later rains would come. If Jesus' ascension into heaven produced the early rains and an early harvest in the nations, how much more will His return to the earth produce the later rains and the greater harvest?

The labor of the church for two thousand years can be compared to the labor of a farmer preparing the ground of harvest. Just as the early rain in ancient Israel enabled farmers to labor for the great harvest, so also the outpouring of the Spirit we enjoy enables us to work for a great coming harvest.

The Bible repeatedly describes the end times as the time when the harvest is gathered in from the earth. With the recent explosion of population in the earth, a global revival could easily produce more Christians on the planet than are in heaven, and this makes sense of the passages that described God harvesting His people from the earth. *Unfortunately, some in the church have seen the end times only as a time of unsurpassed trouble, but biblically it is also the time of harvest.*

Even Israel's full salvation will not come until the fullness (harvest) of the Gentiles (nations) comes in:

> *Lest you be wise in your own sight, I do not want you to be unaware of this mystery, brothers: a partial hardening has come upon Israel, until the fullness of the Gentiles has come in. (Romans 11:25)*

To understand the end times correctly, we must understand it is a time of harvest. Not only will Israel come to salvation at this time, the harvest from the nations will also be gathered in.

God's End-Time Signs and Wonders

As we saw earlier, the Bible predicts a coming second Exodus—a time when God delivers His people in power and does something so dramatic it causes people to no longer refer to Him as the God of the Exodus.[6] If God is going to release His power in the nations on behalf of Israel in a way that far exceeds what He did in the Exodus, it has significant implications for how we understand what God is going to do in and through His people.

Jesus has brought together Jew and Gentile into one body and grafted the Gentiles into Israel.[7] Therefore, when God releases His end-time power, it will affect every part of Jesus' body. The promise of a second Exodus means all God's people—both Jew and Gentile—will experience an unprecedented demonstration of God's power.

In the Exodus, God demonstrated His absolute control over creation and, in the process, destroyed the most powerful empire in the earth. It is hard for us to imagine the events of the Exodus, but the Bible tells us God's end-time activity will be so profound it cannot be compared to the Exodus. *God released His power in the ancient Exodus on*

---

[6] See Isaiah 4:5; 11:11–12, 16; 64:1–3; Jeremiah 16:14; 23:6–7.

[7] See Romans 11:17; Ephesians 2:12–13.

behalf of His people, and He will also release His end-time power on behalf of His people.

In the book of Acts, as opposition increased against the gospel, God released supernatural power to advance the gospel. This is a pattern that helps us to understand the end-time church. *If God released unusual power to establish the church amid Roman opposition, how much more will He release great power on the church to resist the most evil man in history and Satan's great rage?*

Revelation 11 gives us a small picture of the power God will release during this time in history:

> *"And I will grant authority to my two witnesses, and they will prophesy for twelve hundred and sixty days, clothed in sackcloth." These are the two olive trees and the two lampstands that stand before the Lord of the earth. And if anyone wants to harm them, fire flows out of their mouth and devours their enemies; so if anyone wants to harm them, he must be killed in this way. These have the power to shut up the sky, so that rain will not fall during the days of their prophesying; and they have power over the waters to turn them into blood, and to strike the earth with every plague, as often as they desire. (vv. 3–6 NASB)*

Though the two witnesses in Revelation 11 are mysterious, the message is clear: *God will release dramatic power on His people during the end times to accomplish His purposes.* These two witnesses will be in Jerusalem as a statement of God's commitment to Israel. They will "prophesy" accompanied by power. In the same way, the end-time church will proclaim the gospel with unusual signs and wonders. This shows us why Jesus predicted that "greater works" were available for the church:

> *Truly, truly, I say to you, he who believes in Me, the works that I do, he will do also; and greater works than these he will do; because I go to the Father. (John 14:12 NASB)*

Revelation 12 also describes the intensity of the end times:

> *Then I heard a loud voice in heaven, saying, "Now the salvation, and the power, and the kingdom of our God and the authority of His Christ have come, for the accuser of our brethren has been thrown down, he who accuses them before our God day and night. "And they overcame him because of the blood of the Lamb and because of the word of their*

testimony, and they did not love their life even when faced with death. "For this reason, rejoice, O heavens and you who dwell in them. Woe to the earth and the sea, because the devil has come down to you, having great wrath, knowing that he has only a short time." (vv. 10–12 NASB)

The end-time church will be marked by martyrdom because there will be those within her who will "not love their lives to the death." This is a statement of maturity. The situation on the earth will be severe because the devil will have great wrath since he realizes his time is short. However, at the same time the earth suffers the effects of Satan's end-time rage, heaven rejoices because the salvation and power of God are being released. God will release power and glory to match Satan's rage.

Isaiah tells us God's glory will rest on His people in the middle of the end-time trouble:

"For behold, darkness will cover the earth and deep darkness the peoples; but the Lord will rise upon you and His glory will appear upon you." (Isaiah 60:2 NASB)

All of these promises have massive implications for how we think about the end-time church. The church in the end times is never presented as a tiny remnant barely surviving. The end times are a climax of both negative and positive dynamics, and by examining everything the Bible says about the end-time church, we can easily conclude God will release the most powerful signs and wonders at the end of the age.

KEY CHARACTERISTICS OF THE END-TIME CHURCH

When we consider the descriptions of the end-time church we have examined so far, we can identify three key characteristics:

1. She will be mature.
2. She will be of significant size.
3. She will be global in that there will be a victorious church in every people group.

There is another characteristic of the end-time church we should examine: The Bible repeatedly predicts extravagant worship and prayer will be characteristic of the end-time church. This is another biblical indicator of the maturity and size of the end-time church. Only a significant harvest of the kind Revelation 7:9–17 implies could produce the extravagant worship and prayer the Bible predicts.

Worship and prayer are normal in the church, but the worship and prayer of the end-time church will be on an unusual scale and have a global scope. It will be so profound it will challenge the Antichrist.

Extravagant Worship with Prayer

Worship may be described as *agreement with who God is* while *prayer* may be defined as *agreement with what God wants to do*. When we look at the end-time songs and prayers of the church, they contain both of these elements. Some verses highlight worship while others highlight prayer, but together these passages give us a picture of the end-time church.

Over the last several decades, worship and prayer have increasingly come together in the church as a single expression that celebrates who

God is and agrees with what He wants to do in the earth. This is a foreshadowing of what the prophets predicted.

One of the most striking predictions of the end-time church in Revelation 22:17 is that a day will come when the Spirit and the bride say, "Come." That single phrase *come* encapsulates a global cry for the return of Jesus. That cry is not unique to the book of Revelation. The Bible repeatedly describes a global cry that will emerge on the earth before Jesus returns.[1] This global cry will be one of the most vivid expressions of God's triumph over Satan.

In the garden, Satan convinced man to reject God. However, a great cry is going to erupt in the earth. It will be a cry of invitation for God to return to the earth and a cry of desire for the Son of God to return.

The church will take her place in the nations as one human voice and invite the Son of God to take over the earth. What makes this cry even more majestic is that it will come during the darkest hour of history. It will reach its climax during the reign of the Antichrist, and it will be a beautiful, global expression of love and devotion to Jesus. It will be the cry of a bride who is no longer content with separation from her bridegroom. The cry of the end-time church is one of the Father's great gifts to His Son, and Jesus will answer that cry with His majestic return.[2]

The psalmist commanded the nations to sing in light of the Lord's return because the Father wants His Son welcomed with joyful and extravagant singing. These Psalms are instructions to be obeyed, but they are more than that. They are prophecies of a global church who will sing about the coming of the Lord.[3]

Ascribe to the Lord, O families of the peoples, ascribe to the Lord glory and strength. Ascribe to the Lord the glory of His name; bring an

---

[1] The Bible repeatedly commands the nations to worship God, and it describes and predicts extravagant worship and prayer in the nations. See Psalm 96:1, 9, 13; 98:1–9; 102:15–22; 122:6; 149:6–9; Isaiah 19:20–22; 24:14–16; 25:9; 26:1, 8–9; 27:2–5, 13; 30:18–19, 29, 32; 35:2, 10; 42:10–15; 43:26; 51:11; 52:8; 62:6–7; Jeremiah 31:7; Joel 2:12–17, 32; Zephaniah 2:1–3; Zechariah 8:20–23; 10:1; 12:10; 13:9; Matthew 21:13; Luke 18:7–8; Romans 15:8–11; Revelation 5:8; 8:3–5; 16:7; 22:17.

[2] See Isaiah 42:10–14.

[3] The Psalms are frequently treated as prophecy in the New Testament.

offering and come into His courts. Worship the Lord in holy attire; tremble before Him, all the earth. Say among the nations, "The Lord reigns; indeed, the world is firmly established, it will not be moved; He will judge the peoples with equity." Let the heavens be glad, and let the earth rejoice; let the sea roar, and all it contains; let the field exult, and all that is in it. Then all the trees of the forest will sing for joy before the Lord, for He is coming, for He is coming to judge the earth. He will judge the world in righteousness and the peoples in His faithfulness. (Psalm 96:7–13 NASB)

O sing to the Lord a new song, for He has done wonderful things, His right hand and His holy arm have gained the victory for Him. The Lord has made known His salvation; He has revealed His righteousness in the sight of the nations. He has remembered His lovingkindness and His faithfulness to the house of Israel; all the ends of the earth have seen the salvation of our God. Shout joyfully to the Lord, all the earth; break forth and sing for joy and sing praises. Sing praises to the Lord with the lyre, with the lyre and the sound of melody. With trumpets and the sound of the horn shout joyfully before the King, the Lord. Let the sea roar and all it contains, the world and those who dwell in it. Let the rivers clap their hands, let the mountains sing together for joy before the Lord, for He is coming to judge the earth; He will judge the world with righteousness and the peoples with equity. (Psalm 98 NASB)

Isaiah prophesied the fulfillment of Psalm 93 and 96 when he predicted extravagant worship in the nations during the end-times:

The earth mourns and withers; the world languishes and withers; the highest people of the earth languish. . . . Therefore a curse devours the earth, and its inhabitants suffer for their guilt; therefore the inhabitants of the earth are scorched, and few men are left. . . . The wine mourns, the vine languishes, all the merry-hearted sigh. The mirth of the tambourines is stilled, the noise of the jubilant has ceased, the mirth of the lyre is stilled. No more do they drink wine with singing; strong drink is bitter to those who drink it. . . . Desolation is left in the city; the gates are battered into ruins. For thus it shall be in the midst of the earth among the nations, as when an olive tree is beaten, as at the gleaning when the grape harvest is done. They lift up their voices, they sing for joy; over the majesty of the Lord they shout from the west. Therefore in the east give glory to the Lord; in the coastlands of the sea, give glory to the name of the Lord, the God of Israel. From the ends of the earth we hear songs of praise, of glory to the Righteous One. (Isaiah 24:4, 6, 7–9, 12–16)

Isaiah's description of the end times is extraordinary. First, Isaiah explained deep darkness will cover the earth during the reign of the Antichrist. Songs will cease. Celebration will cease. Even the powerful people of the earth will suffer. In the middle of this unparalleled time of trouble and great darkness,[4] Isaiah predicted that songs will suddenly erupt in the nations. Isaiah forecasted songs will come from the very ends of the earth, declaring the glory of God in the midst of the darkest hour of human history.

These prophecies are fulfilled by the end-time church and, therefore, are a profound statement of the end-time church's maturity. The Antichrist will not be able to overcome this church. Instead the church will challenge him by releasing her songs. God will use these end-time songs to release courage across the nations. The fact that these songs are heard across the earth means the end-time church is a significant force in the earth. This is the great multitude that John could not number in Revelation 7:9. When no one else has hope, the church will have hope. When no one else sings, she will sing proclamations of the beauty of God.

Isaiah prophesied this end-time expression of extravagant worship again in Isaiah 42:

Sing to the Lord a new song, sing His praise from the end of the earth! You who go down to the sea, and all that is in it. You islands, and those who dwell on them. Let the wilderness and its cities lift up their voices, the settlements where Kedar inhabits. Let the inhabitants of Sela sing aloud, let them shout for joy from the tops of the mountains. Let them give glory to the Lord and declare His praise in the coastlands. The Lord will go forth like a warrior, He will arouse His zeal like a man of war. He will utter a shout, yes, He will raise a war cry. He will prevail against His enemies. "I have kept silent for a long time, I have kept still and restrained Myself. Now like a woman in labor I will groan, I will both gasp and pant. I will lay waste the mountains and hills and wither all

---

[4] See Jeremiah 30:7; Daniel 12:1; Joel 2:2; Matthew 24:21.

their vegetation; I will make the rivers into coastlands and dry up the ponds. (vv. 10–15 NASB)

Isaiah 42 tells us that Jesus' return is a response to a cry of worship and intercession on the earth. The chapter begins with the prediction of the beauty of God's Servant (Jesus). In light of the beauty of God's Servant, Isaiah commanded the nations to sing from the very ends of the earth and associated this extravagant singing with the return of the Lord. In response, Jesus will release His own cry that is compared to the cry of a "woman in labor." The strength of Jesus' response tells us quite a bit about the strength of the church's cry. *God will cry out in His strength because the church will have cried out in hers.*

In both Isaiah 24 and 42, the prophet predicted extravagant worship and prayer that are connected to the return of Jesus and will reach a climax during the rule of the Antichrist. This end-time church will not only be a witness in the nations, but she will also be a strength to Israel. Isaiah summarizes this in chapter 62:

> *For Zion's sake I will not keep silent, and for Jerusalem's sake I will not keep quiet, until her righteousness goes forth like brightness, and her salvation like a torch that is burning. The nations will see your righteousness, and all kings your glory; and you will be called by a new name which the mouth of the Lord will designate. . . . On your walls, O Jerusalem, I have appointed watchmen; all day and all night they will never keep silent. You who remind the Lord, take no rest for yourselves; and give Him no rest until He establishes and makes Jerusalem a praise in the earth. . . . Behold, the Lord has proclaimed to the end of the earth, say to the daughter of Zion, "Lo, your salvation comes; behold His reward is with Him, and His recompense before Him." And they will call them, "The holy people, the redeemed of the Lord"; And you will be called, "Sought out, a city not forsaken." (vv. 62:1–2, 6–7, 11–12 NASB)*

This is a message for the end-time church. God will not be silent with regard to the future of Jerusalem because the nations are going to see the glory and wonder of His salvation in Israel. When God says He will not be silent, He is inviting us to not be silent, too. We are to be like watchmen. Watchmen look for what is coming. We know what is coming because of the Scriptures. In light of those Scriptures, we are to cry out and give the Lord "no rest" until He fulfills His promises.

In Isaiah 62:11–12, God commands the nations to declare His promises to Israel. This is part of the calling of the end-time church in the nations. God will not be silent, so we will not be silent. He cannot rest until His purposes are accomplished, and He invites us to raise up a sound that will not allow Him to rest. This is an invitation to intercession. *God is asking the church for intercession that will not stop until He accomplishes everything He wants to do.*

This is an invitation to us to play a significant role in God's fulfillment of His promises. God does not give this kind of invitation unless He knows His people will respond to it. Therefore, the invitation of Isaiah 62 is ultimately a prophecy of the mature church. A time will come when the earth is filled with ceaseless intercession until God executes all His promises, and God will release His end-time deliverance in response to our prayers.

The Church—A Priestly People in the Nations

Malachi also predicted that God would receive extravagant worship from the nations:

> *"For from the rising of the sun even to its setting, My name will be great among the nations, and in every place incense is going to be offered to My name, and a grain offering that is pure; for My name will be great among the nations," says the Lord of hosts. (1:11 NASB)*

Malachi predicted worship will fill the nations so that God's name will be great in *every place.* God is not willing to surrender any part of the earth. Worship will fill every part. He is also unwilling to surrender any part of the day. Worship will occur from the beginning to the end of the day. *Malachi predicted worship would fill the nations in an extravagant way—something far beyond a weekly meeting or an hour here and there.*

The context of Malachi 1 makes this prophecy even more profound. Malachi 1 described Israel's failure to operate as a priestly people. God provoked Israel in this chapter with the prediction that He was going to establish worship and priestly ministry in all the nations.

This prediction reveals two key things about the end-time church. *First, the worship of the nations is connected to the recovery of Israel's priestly calling.* By being a priestly people in the nations, the church will play a part in God's plan to call Israel back to her priestly calling. This is part of what Paul refers to as God's plan to provoke Israel through the Gentiles.[5]

Second, it means that Israel's priestly ministry is a prototype of what God is going to raise up in the nations. The worship ministry God established in Israel was extravagant. It went day and night. It was the central function of the nation. In the same way, the ministry of worship and intercession will become central in the church. It will be extravagant. It will be night and day, just as it was in Israel. *The risen Jesus is not worthy of less adoration than He was in the Old Testament.*

The entire nation of Israel was priestly,[6] just as the entire church is priestly,[7] but specific individuals within Israel made the maintenance of night-and-day worship their full-time, primary vocation. In the same way, there will be people in the church who maintain night-and-day worship and prayer as their full-time vocation. We have had full-time Christian workers throughout history, and it will take full-time singers and musicians to fulfill what the prophets have predicted.

Jesus' Desire for Extravagant Worship and Prayer

As Jesus answered questions about His return in Luke 17:22–37, He described how dramatic that day will be:

> *For as the lightning flashes and lights up the sky from one side to the other, so will the Son of Man be in his day. (v. 24)*

He then gave a parable with instructions on how to prepare for His return:

> *Now He was telling them a parable to show that at all times they ought to pray and not to lose heart, saying, "In a certain city there was a judge who did not fear God and did not respect man. There was a widow in that city, and she kept coming to him, saying, 'Give me legal protection from my opponent.' For a while he was unwilling; but afterward he said to himself, 'Even though I do not fear God nor respect man, yet because this widow bothers me, I will give her legal protection, otherwise by continually*

---

[5] See Romans 11:11.

[6] See Exodus 19:6.

[7] See 1 Peter 2:9; Revelation 1:6; 5:10; 20:6.

coming she will wear me out.'" And the Lord said, "Hear what the unrighteous judge said; now, will not God bring about justice for His elect who cry to Him day and night, and will He delay long over them? I tell you that He will bring about justice for them quickly. However, when the Son of Man comes, will He find faith on the earth?" (Luke 18:1–8 NASB)

In the parable, Jesus highlighted the constant intercession of a widow looking for justice. She would not stop, so she continued to ask an unwilling judge for what she wanted until she got it. Jesus ended the parable with the question, "When the Son of Man comes, will He find faith on the earth?" Faith, in this context, is the consistent intercession of the widow. Luke told us the point of the parable was that we should always pray and not lose heart. In light of the context, the parable emphasized extravagant intercession as part of preparing for Jesus' return.

The scene in the parable communicates two key aspects of what it means to have faith. The first is that we ask and keep on asking. The parable is an invitation to the church to engage in constant intercession. Jesus uses the example of a widow in the parable because a widow has no other option. She does not have any resources to depend on if her requests are not answered. The message for us is clear: *Our only real solution is found in securing the resources of God in the place of prayer.*

The second main point is that we will get what we ask when we come in confidence. Jesus knows that it will seem, at times, as if God is not listening or answering. He knows the end-time church will especially face this temptation when she sees the Antichrist rise to power. However, His message to the church is to keep asking with confidence that God will answer. Jesus ends the parable with an invitation for the end-time church. He is looking for a mature church operating in faith, and the parable gives instructions to the church on how to be the church Jesus will find when He returns.

Jesus also asked us to pray that the earth would become like heaven:

"Pray, then, in this way: 'Our Father who is in heaven, Hallowed be Your name. Your kingdom come. Your will be done, on earth as it is in heaven.'" (Matthew 6:9–10 NASB)

When John was caught up in Revelation 4 through 5, he gave us an idea of what God's will being done in heaven will look like. John saw the glory of God in the midst of an extravagant expression of intercession and worship. He saw the living creatures cry out because of the glory of God and elders who carry harps (music) and bowls full of the saints' prayers (intercession). John's glimpse into heaven in Revelation 4 through 5 gives us a picture of what Jesus asked us to pray for, and when the Father's will is done on the earth as it is in heaven, the earth will be filled with the same worship ministry that currently exists in heaven.

Paul's Mission to Establish Worship and Prayer

Paul labored among the Gentiles to see a great expression of worship erupt in the nations. In Romans 15, he quoted Old Testament passages[8] describing Israel's worship ministry and applied them to the Gentiles because he understood the centrality of worship in ancient Israel was meant to be a pattern for the church. The expression of priestly ministry in the Old Testament Tabernacle and the Temple point towards a greater expression in the church.

> *For I say that Christ has become a servant to the circumcision on behalf of the truth of God to confirm the promises given to the fathers, and for the Gentiles to glorify God for His mercy; as it is written, "THEREFORE I WILL GIVE PRAISE TO YOU AMONG THE GENTILES, AND I WILL SING TO YOUR NAME." Again he says, "REJOICE, O GENTILES, WITH HIS PEOPLE." And again, "PRAISE THE LORD ALL YOU GENTILES, AND LET ALL THE PEOPLES PRAISE HIM." Again Isaiah says, "THERE SHALL COME THE ROOT OF JESSE, AND HE WHO ARISES TO RULE OVER THE GENTILES, IN HIM SHALL THE GENTILES HOPE." (Romans 15:8–12 NASB)*

Antioch was the first significant church in the nations, and Luke's description of that church emphasizes this foundation:

---

[8] See 2 Samuel 22:50; Deuteronomy 32:43; Psalm 18:49; 117:1.

Now there were at Antioch, in the church that was there, prophets and teachers: Barnabas, and Simeon who was called Niger, and Lucius of Cyrene, and Manaen who had been brought up with Herod the tetrarch, and Saul. While they were ministering to the Lord and fasting, the Holy Spirit said, "Set apart for Me Barnabas and Saul for the work to which I have called them." (Acts 13:1–2 NASB)

The word *ministering* in Acts 13:2 is the same word that was used to refer to temple ministry. David Peterson wrote the following about Acts 13:

Since the Lord is the object of service or ministry here, Luke may be suggesting that corporate prayer is the "cultic" activity which replaces the sacrificial approach to God which was at the heart of Judaism.[9]

Up to this point, Jerusalem had been the center of worship to the God of Israel, but the temple was going to be destroyed within a few decades. Therefore, Antioch was presented by Luke as the model of what church would look like in the nations. The priestly ministry was not eliminated as the gospel spread into the nations. It was expanded. Each congregation is a small "temple" where the people of God stand as priests and minister to God. The apostle Paul was launched into the nations to reproduce this kind of church throughout the gentile world.

John Piper summarized the mission of the church with his well-known statement in his book on missions:

Missions is not the ultimate goal of the Church. Worship is. Missions exists because worship doesn't. Worship is ultimate, not missions, because God is ultimate, not man. When this age is over, and the countless millions of the redeemed fall on their faces before the throne of God, missions will be no more. It is a temporary necessity. But worship abides forever.[10]

---

[9] David G. Peterson, *The Acts of the Apostles*, The Pillar New Testament Commentary (Grand Rapids, MI; Nottingham, England: William B. Eerdmans Publishing Company, 2009), 375.

[10] John Piper, *Let the Nations Be Glad! The Supremacy of God in Missions* (Grand Rapids: Baker, 1993/2003), 17.

This is God's ultimate goal for world missions. We are called to do more than evangelize and plant churches. We are called to labor for extravagant worship in the nations.

The Intercession of the Mature End-Time Church

The prophets predicted worship in the nations, Jesus died for it, and the apostles labored for it. Therefore, we can be guaranteed history is building up to a moment when the nations release extravagant songs of praise. When the book of Revelation describes every tribe and tongue, they are in the place of worship and intercession:

And they sang a new song, saying, "Worthy are you to take the scroll and to open its seals, for you were slain, and by your blood you ransomed people for God from every tribe and language and people and nation, and you have made them a kingdom and priests to our God, and they shall reign on the earth." (5:9–10)

After this I looked, and behold, a great multitude that no one could number, from every nation, from all tribes and peoples and languages, standing before the throne and before the Lamb, clothed in white robes, with palm branches in their hands, and crying out with a loud voice, "Salvation belongs to our God who sits on the throne, and to the Lamb!" (7:9–10)

The message is clear. The mature church in every tribe and tongue will emerge in the end times, and when she emerges, she will release a profound cry. That cry will be global, coming from every people group. The church will declare the beauty and majesty of Jesus and function in her priestly identity before the Lord.

The book of Revelation also tells us the intercession of the church will set God's end-time activity into motion:

And another angel came and stood at the altar with a golden censer, and he was given much incense to offer with the prayers of all the saints on the golden altar before the throne, and the smoke of the incense, with the prayers of the saints, rose before God from the hand of the angel. Then the angel took the censer and filled it with fire from the altar and threw it on the earth, and there were peals of thunder, rumblings, flashes of lightning, and an earthquake. (8:3–5)

And they sing the song of Moses, the servant of God, and the song of the Lamb, saying, "Great and amazing are your deeds, O Lord God the Almighty! Just and true are your ways, O King of the nations!" (15:3)

Extravagant prayer is captured in heaven and combined with God's activity to activate His end-time plan. John was given this vision to give us courage to obey Luke 18. When it seems like our prayers are not being answered, God is collecting them, and they will play a part in releasing His activity. The end-time church is confident singing of the glory of God and interceding for God's purposes. These passages give us a picture of the end-time church in order to provoke us to confident, bold intercession.

Worship and the Church—The Biblical Pattern

Songs and prayers naturally come to human beings, so when the Bible predicts extravagant worship and prayer, it is predicting something beyond what we currently consider to be "normal." The prophets predicted something with a global impact during the reign of the Antichrist.

They predicted a sound that could not be silenced when all other human songs will go silent. They heard songs that would give hope to the nations, describe the glory of God, and strengthen Israel during the end-time crisis. The prophets saw something extravagant, global, mature, and impossible to ignore. They heard and predicted a global cry— something we have not yet seen or heard. It will take a mature church to resist the Antichrist and release these kinds of songs during the end times. That church will be significant enough that the nations will be provoked by her songs.

When God began His redemptive plan with Israel, the first thing He did—before He even gave her a land—was to establish a worship ministry at the very center of the nation. He put priests in place, not simply to manage sacrifices, but to maintain night-and-day worship.[11] He called the entire nation, not only the vocational priests, to be a

---

[11] Symbolized by the daily burning of incense, lamps, and the showbread. See Exodus 25:30, 37; 30:1.

priestly nation.[12] This emphasis on worship is a foreshadowing of God's ultimate intention for the church.

King David was the greatest King of Israel and one of the primary prototypes of the Messiah. God loved David's heart so much that He made an unconditional promise that the Messiah would be David's Son.[13] David's burden for night-and-day worship and the presence of God among His people is one of the reasons David is referred to as a man after God's heart.[14]

Before he was a king, David was a shepherd who spent a lot of time alone, and David used this time to minister to God and compose songs. *Though David was a shepherd and a king, he was a priest at heart, and that was what qualified Him to be Israel's greatest king.*

When David became king, he was driven by a desire to build a "resting place" on the earth for the Lord's presence:

> *Remember, O Lord, on David's behalf, all his affliction; how he swore to the Lord and vowed to the Mighty One of Jacob, "Surely I will not enter my house, nor lie on my bed; I will not give sleep to my eyes or slumber to my eyelids, until I find a place for the Lord, a dwelling place for the Mighty One of Jacob." (Psalm 132:1–5 NASB)*

> *"David found favor in God's sight, and asked that he might find a dwelling place for the God of Jacob." (Acts 7:46 NASB)*

As the church, we long for the return of Jesus and the time God will dwell physically on the earth among His people. Until that day comes, God dwells among His people in the context of night-and-day worship.[15] David understood this, and this is why the most unique characteristic of David's rule was what we refer to as *David's Tabernacle.* It was a worship sanctuary where David took the Ark of the Covenant, which represented God's presence among His people, and he put it in a tabernacle and set in place singers and musicians to sing night and day about the glory of God.

---

[12] See Exodus 19:6.

[13] See 2 Samuel 7:8–17.

[14] See 1 Samuel 13:14; Acts 13:22.

[15] See Psalm 9:11; 22:3; 65:1; 102:21; 147:12.

What we must understand about David's tabernacle is that it was a prophetic expression of God's intention. David was demonstrating something that would come in the future. There were no sacrifices in David's Tabernacle, only night-and-day worship. It was an expression of a new reality that was coming, and that new reality has a New Testament manifestation.

The reformers in Israel who came after David understood the significance of this worship ministry and reestablished it as part of their reforms.[16] John the Baptist taught his disciples to pray, and the disciples asked Jesus to teach them to pray because of how central it was to who Jesus was.[17]

When the church began, there was night-and-day worship at the temple, and the early church in Jerusalem valued the ministry happening at the temple.[18] The book of Acts shows the early church gave a primary place to corporate worship and prayer.[19] Paul instructed the churches to sing spiritual songs to each other and labored for an expressive, singing church.[20] All of these were prototypes of what is coming, and the end of the age is the time when God brings the fulfillment of the types and shadows of the Old Testament.

---

[16] See 2 Chronicles 8:14–15; 20:19–22, 28; 23:1; 24:27; 29:1–36; 30:21; 35:1–27; Ezra 3:10–11; Nehemiah 12:24–47.

[17] See Luke 11:1.

[18] See Acts 3:11; 5:12.

[19] See Acts 1:14; 4:24–31; 6:4; 12:12; 13:1–3; 16:25; 20:36.

[20] See Romans 15:8–11; Ephesians 5:19; Colossians 3:16.

Part 5: War Over the Promises

THE END-TIME CONFLICT

We began by looking at God's promises and how they set the stage for the end times. After that, we examined Israel's covenantal crisis and God's plan to resolve it. We followed that by looking at some of the descriptions of the end-time church to better grasp what the fulfillment of God's promise to the nations will look like. Each of these sections help make sense of the end-time drama because the end times are simply the logical conclusion to God's redemptive plan in this age.

In this final section, we will examine the main reasons for the coming end-time conflict which will be a war over the promises of God. When we look at the passages in the Bible describing end-time events, many of them seem to revolve around the city of Jerusalem, a great conflict over the Jewish people, and God's dramatic salvation of the Jewish people. To understand this conflict, we must know why Israel is so central in the end-time events and what role the gentile church is called to play during them.

Through Jesus, God has brought the Gentiles into Israel's story, and as a result, the global church has a specific role to play related to Israel during the end-time crisis.[1] The story of Israel and the nations has always been one story. Our salvation is connected to her salvation. Our future is connected to her future. Therefore, Israel's trouble is also our trouble. This is true now but will be especially true at the end of the age.

God is going to bring His family together from Israel and the nations. He will bring the Jewish people to a point where they love the nations and desire to serve them. He will also cause the gentile church to identify with Israel and Israel's Jewish King.

---

[1] See Ephesians 2:12–13; Romans 11:17.

The Church Is Joined to Israel's Story

Hebrews addresses how the body of Jesus is to function as one body. When we truly become one body, we naturally rejoice with those who rejoice and weep with those who weep whether or not they are part of our natural family:[2]

> *Remember those who are in prison, as though in prison with them, and those who are mistreated, since you also are in the body. (13:3)*

Hebrews 13:3 is an instruction for the body of Jesus, but it also represents a principle for how the gentile church relates to Israel.[3] While we are only family with those who have embraced Jesus, we have been joined to Israel's story. Furthermore, as we have seen, the rage of the enemy against Israel is ultimately an expression of his rage against Jesus.

Therefore, whenever Israel suffers, there is a sense in which the gentile church participates in that suffering when she stands in agreement with God's covenantal promises. We saw this on a small scale during the Holocaust. Faithful gentile believers suffered for standing with the Jewish people, but a much bigger storm is coming.

Why Is Israel so Central in End-Time Events?

Israel is central in end-time events because of the specific promises God made to her that He must accomplish to be true to His Word. Let's review a few key passages.

God promised to preserve the nation of Israel forever, boldly stating that if He could not uphold her He could not uphold creation:[4]

> *Thus says the Lord, who gives the sun for light by day and the fixed order of the moon and the stars for light by night, who stirs up the sea so that its waves roar; the Lord of hosts is His name: "If this fixed order departs from before Me," declares the Lord, "Then the offspring of Israel also will cease from being a nation before Me forever." Thus says the Lord, "If the heavens above can be measured and the foundations of the earth searched out below, then I will also cast off all the offspring of*

---

[2] See also Romans 12:15; 1 Corinthians 12:26.

[3] See Romans 11:18–24.

[4] See also Isaiah 66:22–23; 65:17–19.

Israel for all that they have done," declares the Lord. (Jeremiah 31:35–37 NASB)

The word of the Lord came to Jeremiah, saying, "Thus says the Lord, 'If you can break My covenant for the day and My covenant for the night, so that day and night will not be at their appointed time, then My covenant may also be broken with David My servant so that he will not have a son to reign on his throne, and with the Levitical priests, My ministers. As the host of heaven cannot be counted and the sand of the sea cannot be measured, so I will multiply the descendants of David My servant and the Levites who minister to Me.'" And the word of the Lord came to Jeremiah, saying, "Have you not observed what this people have spoken, saying, 'The two families which the Lord chose, He has rejected them'? Thus they despise My people, no longer are they as a nation in their sight. "Thus says the Lord, 'If My covenant for day and night stand not, and the fixed patterns of heaven and earth I have not established, then I would reject the descendants of Jacob and David My servant, not taking from his descendants rulers over the descendants of Abraham, Isaac and Jacob. But I will restore their fortunes and will have mercy on them.'" (33:19–26 NASB)

Furthermore, Jesus predicted He would not return to rule and reign without saving Israel. In Matthew 23:39, Jesus told the rulers of Jerusalem that He would not rule over them until they said to Him, "Blessed is He who comes in the name of the Lord":

"O Jerusalem, Jerusalem, the city that kills the prophets and stones those who are sent to it! How often would I have gathered your children together as a hen gathers her brood under her wings, and you were not willing! . . . For I tell you, you will not see me again, until you say, 'Blessed is he who comes in the name of the Lord.'" (Matthew 23:37, 39)

In Matthew 24:30 Jesus quoted Zechariah 12:10–12 to predict that His second coming would be a time when Israel's eyes were opened and they embraced Him as Messiah. Acts 1:6–8 makes it clear Jesus promised the apostles He would save and restore Israel. Peter preached that Jesus would return to save and restore Israel.[5]

---

[5] See Acts 3:20–21.

Jesus' return sets into motion His judgments on the nations and on Satan and his kingdom. Therefore, the enemy's primary strategy is to do everything possible to prevent the day of Christ's return and the release of His judgments. Jesus' return is associated with the fulfillment of Israel's promises; therefore, the enemy will do everything he can to prevent the fulfillment of these promises and the return of Jesus. *During the end times, the powers of evil are not simply persecuting God's people; they are fighting for their own survival.*

A Summary of the End-Time Conflict

Revelation 12 provides one of the clearest and most concise descriptions of the coming end-time conflict. The chapter begins with a description of a woman giving birth to a child:

> *And a great sign appeared in heaven: a woman clothed with the sun, with the moon under her feet, and on her head a crown of twelve stars. She was pregnant and was crying out in birth pains and the agony of giving birth. (12:1–2)*

This woman with a crown of twelve stars symbolizes Israel and the struggle of her history. John saw her ready to give birth, and then suddenly he saw something gruesome:

> *And another sign appeared in heaven: behold, a great red dragon, with seven heads and ten horns, and on his heads seven diadems. . . . And the dragon stood before the woman who was about to give birth, so that when she bore her child he might devour it. (Revelation 12:3–4)*

A great red dragon appeared and stood before the woman in order to eat her child. The dragon was fixated on the woman because of her child.

> *She gave birth to a male child, one who is to rule all the nations with a rod of iron, but her child was caught up to God and to his throne. (v. 5)*

Though the dragon tried to destroy the woman, she gave birth to a male child. It is the child—the Messiah—who is to rule the nations with the rod of iron.[6] However, the Messiah was suddenly caught up to the throne. The imagery up to this point is clear. The woman with

---

[6] See Psalm 2:9; Revelation 2:27; 19:15.

twelve stars represents Israel who the Lord chose to "give birth" to the Messiah. The Messiah is the male child who has been born but then caught up to the throne of God in the ascension. The rage of the dragon against the woman was because of the child.

The dragon, which is Satan,[7] cannot make war on Jesus because Jesus has been caught up to the heavens and is seated at the right hand of the throne of God.[8] Because he cannot challenge the throne of God, he chooses to wage war on the earth. He does that right now as he attempts to deceive and seduce the nations,[9] but something bigger is coming. Revelation 12 tells us a day is coming when Satan will be cast down to the earth and will be in a rage because he knows his time is short:[10]

> *And the great dragon was thrown down, the serpent of old who is called the devil and Satan, who deceives the whole world; he was thrown down to the earth, and his angels were thrown down with him. . . . "For this reason, rejoice, O heavens and you who dwell in them. Woe to the earth and the sea, because the devil has come down to you, having great wrath, knowing that he has only a short time." And when the dragon saw that he was thrown down to the earth, he persecuted the woman who gave birth to the male child. (vv. 9, 12–13 NASB)*

Revelation 12:13 predicts that, when the dragon realizes he has been thrown to the earth and his time is short, the first thing he will do

---

[7] See Revelation 12:9.

[8] See Psalm 110:1; Matthew 22:44; Acts 2:33; 7:55–56; Romans 8:34; Ephesians 1:20; Colossians 3:1; Hebrews 1:3; 8:1; 10:12; 12:2; 1 Peter 3:22; Revelation 3:21.

[9] See 1 Peter 5:8; Revelation 12:9.

[10] It is clear from Revelation 12 that this casting down is a future event. Here are a few reasons: Satan is cast down from his place of accusing the brethren day and night (Revelation 12:10), indicating this is not an ancient fall but a removal from a place he currently occupies. His casting down is associated with a period of *time, times and half.* This is a phrase that comes from Daniel and refers to the final period of the great tribulation (Daniel 7:25; 12:7). When the dragon is cast down and stands on the shores of the sea (Revelation 12:17), the beast of Revelation 13 emerges in a human form with all the power and authority of the dragon (Revelation 13:2–4). This dreadful character is the Antichrist and is also associated with the final period of the great tribulation (Revelation 13:5).

is pursue the woman who gave birth to the male child. This is a warning Israel will be the focus of Satan's end-time rage.

And the serpent poured water like a river out of his mouth after the woman, so that he might cause her to be swept away with the flood. But the earth helped the woman, and the earth opened its mouth and drank up the river which the dragon poured out of his mouth. (vv. 15–16 NASB)

The dragon will release a "flood" against the woman to destroy her, but the woman will be helped by the earth. When the woman is supernaturally preserved, the dragon will become furious and make war with "the rest of her offspring" who are those who "have the testimony of Jesus Christ." *The message is plain: The dragon's end-time rage against the followers of Jesus is connected to his inability to destroy Israel.*

So the dragon was enraged with the woman, and went off to make war with the rest of her children, who keep the commandments of God and hold to the testimony of Jesus. (Revelation 12:17 NASB)

Revelation 12 gives a concise summary of the enemy's end-time strategy, and there are several key points that help us understand what will happen in the end times:

- Satan's (the dragon's) end-time rage will be directed against Israel, and he will release a "flood" against her to destroy her. This tells us Israel is the center of Satan's end-time rage. Other passages also predict this rage against Israel, but Revelation 12 helps us to understand it.

- Satan's rage against Israel is an expression of his rage against Jesus (the male child). We must understand that the rage of the nations against Israel is actually an expression of their rage against Jesus. He is the ultimate controversy, not Israel. Israel's role in God's plan to enthrone Jesus over the nations puts Israel in the center of the end-time conflict.

- The "earth" will help save and preserve the woman. This tells us that Satan's assault will not work in the end. Something will happen on the earth that plays a role in preserving Israel (the woman).

- Satan will become furious when he is unable to destroy Israel. This reminds us that the destruction of the woman is his primary objective.[11]

- Satan will direct his rage against the followers of Jesus when he is unable to destroy Israel. This tells us that the followers of Jesus have a role in God's end-time preservation of Israel. Revelation 12 tells us the woman is carried into the wilderness. The wilderness likely represents the nations and their role in serving Israel. This is all part of the earth's preserving the woman.

- Revelation 12 predicts something that has never happened in history: a mature church serving Israel during the most difficult hour of human history. The end-time church will play a role in preventing Satan from destroying Israel as he rages against God's promises.

Note that Israel in this context refers to the people of Israel not necessarily the political nation. God promised Jeremiah He would preserve Israel forever as a people even when Babylon conquered political Israel. Revelation 12 is not focused on the preservation of political Israel (though the prophets tell us the Antichrist will be unable to fully conquer Jerusalem[12]), but the preservation of the people of Israel. This explains why the vision uses a woman to represent Israel. The emphasis is the people.

Revelation 12 gives us a chilling warning: *Satan's final attempt to thwart God's redemptive plan will be an assault on the Jewish people aimed at breaking God's promises.* As believers, we are called to recognize Satan's strategy and prepare for this dark hour of human history. Part of that is preparing to serve the Jewish people even at the cost of our own lives.

---

[11] This assault is so severe that prison camps, captivity, and the subsequent deliverance from these camps are referred to frequently by the prophets. This reveals how systematic the assault will be as well as its scale. See Isaiah 11:11–16; 27:12–13; 42:6–24; 49:5–25; 61:1–2; Jeremiah 30:3–24; 31:1–23; Ezekiel 20:33–44; 39:25–29; Hosea 11:10–11; Amos 9:8–15; Joel 3:1–2; Zephaniah 3:19–20; Zechariah 9:10–14.

[12] See Zechariah 14:2; Revelation 11.

The Enemy's End-Time Rage against Israel

Most Christians assume the church is the primary target of Satan's rage in the final moments of this age, but that is not accurate. The enemy will persecute the church severely, and martyrdom will be a part of the great tribulation,[13] but we need to understand how and why he will focus his rage.

Revelation 12 predicts what all the prophets predicted: Israel will be the center of Satan's end-time rage. (This explains the Bible's repeated predictions that God will release His end-time wrath on the nations on behalf of Israel.[14]) Satan's logic is cold, cruel, and calculating because his primary objective is to break the promises of God and prevent the return of Jesus to prevent his own judgment.

Even if Satan could execute every follower of Jesus—typically estimated to be near two billion people—it would not affect the promises of God or the return of Jesus in any way. In fact, Jesus warned us that we would be hated and would suffer persecution,[15] and the Bible predicts many believers will lose their lives in the end times and inherit great rewards.[16]

However, Israel is something completely different. *If Satan can eliminate the estimated fourteen to fifteen million[17] Jewish people in the earth, then God's promises, including Jesus' promise to return, all break down.* Therefore, the enemy's final, most gruesome assault on the promises of God will include an attempt to eliminate the Jewish people in order to prevent the return of Jesus and the subsequent judgment.

In the end times, the enemy will rage against Israel to the point of seeking Israel's annihilation because it is his most efficient way of attacking God's redemptive plan. It would mean there would be no saved Israel and no Jewish remnant to welcome Jesus and fulfill their role in His return. It would mean

---

[13] See Revelation 6:9; 7:14; 12:11.

[14] See Isaiah 34:1–3, 8; 49:26; 61:2–3; 63:1–9; Joel 3:9–14; Zephaniah 1:14–15; 3:8, 14–15, 17, 19–20; Zechariah 12:2–4; 14:1–5, 9.

[15] See Matthew 10:16–25; Mark 13:9–13; John 16:2, 33.

[16] See Revelation 6:9–10; 7:9–14; 12:11.

[17] DellaPergola, Sergio. "World Jewish Population, 2015," in *The American Jewish Year Book, 2015, Volume 115* (2015). Eds. Arnold Dashefsky and Ira M. Sheskin (Dordrecht: Springer) pp. 273–364.

God was unable to preserve this people as He promised He would. God's final salvation of Israel sets into motion His judgments of the nations, so it would also mean evil in the nations would not be judged. *If the Jewish people ever cease to be a people, and if they are never saved, then Abraham's promises could never be fulfilled, and all of God's promises collapse.*[18]

This is the root of anti-Semitism. Anti-Semitism is more than racism; it is the accusation that the Jews are at the center of the world's problems. This is the position Satan has taken throughout history, and he will take it again at the end of the age because, for him, this will be a true statement. Their redemption will mean his judgment; therefore, as long as Jews exist, they are a statement to God's faithfulness and a key part of God's strategy to bring redemption.

Because the Jewish people set the stage for the return of Jesus and His judgments, Islamists, fascists, humanists, and many others can disagree on virtually everything and yet agree the Jews are the source of the world's problems.

A Graphic and Sober Warning

The Bible's sober prediction of the final conflict over Israel is a warning to us to take the events of the twentieth century seriously—more seriously than we have to this point. The Jewish people have survived persecution (tragically, at times, even at the hands of some people who claimed to be Christians), calamity, and more than an attempt at annihilation. However, the Holocaust is a unique event in history. There was an intensity to the Holocaust that was different when we compare it to Israel's ancient calamities at the hands of Babylon, Rome, and Antiochus.

Both Babylon and Rome were willing to allow the Jewish people to exist with a limited measure of self-rule, so long as they submitted to the dominion of the empire. They only crushed Jerusalem when Jerusalem refused to submit to their rule. Even Antiochus—who was brutal beyond imagination—was driven by his religious and political objectives. Though he became one of the most infamous Antichrist prototypes in history, he rewarded the Jews who were willing to give their loyalty to him and embrace his religion. Babylon, Rome, and Antiochus all sought to destroy Israel when she became an obstacle to

---

[18] See Jeremiah 31:35–37; 33:25–26.

174 IT MUST BE FINISHED

their own agendas. However, none of them saw the elimination of Israel as a core part of seizing their respective destinies.

The Holocaust was completely different. It was not a political conflict over land or submission to a political agenda. When Hitler came to power, the Jewish people could have been a great asset to the German nation. Many were professionals who were committed to Germany's success. Unlike Antiochus, Hitler did not give the Jewish people the chance to declare their loyalty to him. The only option was execution simply because they were Jewish. Even as Hitler's war machine began to fail, he pulled resources back from the front lines to accelerate the work of the death camps. He knew his evil agenda could only succeed if the Jews were eliminated.

God's claim to absolute sovereignty and His redemptive plan all crumble if He is unable to preserve this small people group and bring them into their destiny. Hitler's focus and gruesome tenacity provide a horrific preview of the Antichrist, because he understood he could break the promises of the God of Israel if he could eliminate the Jewish people.

While there have been many antichrists and many Antichrist prototypes through history,[19] Hitler is quite possibly the best picture yet of who the Antichrist will be for several reasons:

- No one expected Hitler's sudden rise to prominence and national power from a relatively unknown beginning. The Bible tells us the Antichrist will initially be considered an insignificant leader and not be given the honor of royalty.[20]

- Hitler was known for his powerful oratory and his mesmerizing speeches. Bold speeches and powerful words are some of the most described characteristics of the Antichrist in the Bible.[21]

- Hitler cast a vision for a thousand-year empire. This was a counterfeit of Jesus' thousand-year rule[22] and an attempt to subvert Jesus as Messiah.

---

[19] See 1 John 2:18.

[20] See Daniel 7:8; 8:9; 11:21.

[21] See Daniel 7:8, 20, 25; 11:36; 2 Thessalonians 2:4; Revelation 13:5–6.

[22] See Revelation 20:3.

- Hitler made the elimination of the Jewish people one of his primary agendas. He believed the elimination of the Jewish people was necessary to achieve his desire to build an evil empire. The Antichrist will also seek their elimination so that he can achieve his objectives.

- Hitler's Holocaust caught an entire nation by surprise. Even at the end of the war, many Germans could not grasp the scope of it. In the same way, the intensity of the end-time conflict over Israel will catch the nations off guard.

- The Holocaust deeply tested the church. The end-time rage against Israel will test the church as well.

- The most chilling part of the Holocaust—referred to as *The Final Solution*—lasted almost precisely the same amount of time the most intense part of the great tribulation will last. During this period, the Nazis accelerated their genocide of the Jewish people. (The first killing center of *The Final Solution* began in December 8, 1941, and the Holocaust ended with the defeat of the Nazis May 8, 1945.[23] This means the most intensive part of the Holocaust lasted one month shy of three and a half years. The Bible repeatedly references the period of three and half years as the duration of the coming great tribulation,[24] and the similarity in time periods is not accidental. It is intended to cause us to pay close attention to World War II.)

In many, ways the Holocaust gives us a gruesome picture of what the Antichrist will attempt. Like Hitler, the coming Antichrist will seek to break God's promises by seeking the end of the Jewish people. It will consume the Antichrist, and he will unleash havoc on the earth in pursuit of this goal, because eliminating the people of Israel would do what nothing else can—break down God's promises by making God a liar who is unable to fulfill what He had promised.

The fact that this gruesome event occurred in our generation at virtually the same time that Israel re-emerged as a sovereign nation

---

[23] United States Holocaust Memorial Museum. "The 'Final Solution.'" Holocaust Encyclopedia. Accessed March 14, 2017. https://www.ushmm.org/outreach/en/article.php?ModuleId=10007704.

[24] See Daniel 7:25; 9:27; 12:7; Revelation 11:2–3; Revelation 13:5.

should cause us to take it very seriously. *If the enemy raged this much over the birth of the modern state of Israel, how much more will he rage over the salvation of the nation?*

Israel has endured trials over the last two thousand years, but we must ask why a trial of this intensity suddenly emerged in our generation at the same time God was setting in motion a historic regathering of Israel to demonstrate His ongoing commitment to her. *We must understand the implications of the accelerating intensity over Israel's salvation and speak boldly with clarity.*

World War II serves as a serious warning to the church. It demonstrates how a crisis centered on Israel is also a test of the church. One of the great tragedies of World War II is that so much of the church did not pass the test of the Holocaust.

World War II illustrates the prediction of Revelation 12 that Satan's rage on Israel will become a rage on the church who stays faithful to what God has said. Though the enemy will set his rage on Israel, the gentile church who has been grafted into Israel will quickly become the object of his rage as well.

Can we honestly say the global church is better prepared than the church was in the last century to survive this kind of test? *Are we actively preparing the church for an event that is similar to the Holocaust and yet surpasses it in ways we cannot imagine?*

Something Unthinkable Is Coming

The Holocaust is a chilling prototype of what the enemy will attempt just before Jesus returns. He will not be silent or passive as he senses the nearness of the return of Jesus and the fulfillment of all God's promises because the fulfillment of those promises sets into motion his judgment.

Satan will answer God's bold, public commitment to His promises as demonstrated in His ongoing redemptive plan for Israel. We simply cannot ignore it or assume that the problem has gone away. *God and His enemy will again contend over Israel's salvation. This time it will be the final, unprecedented conflict over the future of God's promises and the judgment of His enemy.*

God will release supernatural power and preserve the Jewish people, but there will be incredible suffering across the nations for both Jew and Gentile. The entire earth will feel the effects of his rage. This is something the church has very little understanding about and is completely unprepared for.

We cannot conceive of what will happen on the earth when Satan decides to take his final stand and release all his rage against God's promises. World War II was not the final conflict between good and evil. Something far bigger is coming. *The earth has not yet felt the full rage of the enemy against the promises of God.* We have been repeatedly warned that this will be a day like no other day:

> *And it is the time of Jacob's distress, but he will be saved from it. (Jeremiah 30:7 NASB)*

> *There will be a time of distress such as never occurred since there was a nation until that time. (Daniel 12:1 NASB)*

> *A day of darkness and gloom, a day of clouds and thick darkness. As the dawn is spread over the mountains, so there is a great and mighty people; there has never been anything like it, nor will there be again after it. (Joel 2:2 NASB)*

> *For then there will be a great tribulation, such as has not occurred since the beginning of the world until now, nor ever will. (Matthew 24:21 NASB)*

Though Israel has a central place in end-time events, Israel is not the ultimate issue—Jesus is. The enemy will release all his rage against Israel because He is not ultimately fighting Israel—He is making war on Jesus, and God's redemptive plan, through the means he has at his disposal.

Jesus' return as King is an event we can hardly imagine. It will radically reshape everything. When He returns, He will judge the nations, reward righteousness, punish wickedness, and end Satan's present ability to influence and deceive the nations.[25] *The rage of the enemy against Israel in the end times is an expression of how far the enemy will go to try to prevent Jesus' judgment.* Satan's power was broken at the cross,[26] and he cannot dethrone Jesus in the heavens, so the earth will become the final battleground where he will resist Jesus' rule by all means necessary.

---

[25] See Revelation 19:11–20:3.

[26] See Colossians 2:15; Hebrews 2:14–15.

The closer we get to the end, the more desperate our enemy will become. His desperation will center in on Jesus' commitment to save Israel before Jesus takes His throne. He will not only work to keep Israel from the gospel, he also will seek to eliminate her as a people to prevent any possibility of her repentance and Jesus' rule.

JESUS AND THE JUDGMENT OF THE NATIONS

In Matthew 24 through 25, Jesus gave His longest teaching on the end times. This sermon is commonly referred to as the *Olivet Discourse* because Jesus gave it on the Mount of Olives. The teaching has profound implications for how we view the return of Jesus. It emphasizes how significant it is that we understand the key themes.

The teaching can be loosely outlined in this way:

1. Matthew 24:3–14—themes in the nations that will precede the end times.

2. Matthew 24:15–31—key events of the end times.

3. Matthew 24:36–44—instructions about timing and the need to be prepared for Jesus' return.

4. Matthew 24:45–25:30—parables about how to prepare for Jesus' return.

5. Matthew 25:31–46—Jesus' judgment of the nations

There are three keys to understanding this teaching.

1. Treat the entire passage as one sermon.

2. Recognize Jesus' extensive use of Old Testament prophecy.

3. Grasp Jesus' flow as a teacher.

A Single Sermon to Answer a Question

Matthew 24 through 25 is a response to the disciples who were questioning how Jesus would fulfill the predictions of the prophets and initiate His rule over Jerusalem:

As he sat on the Mount of Olives, the disciples came to him privately, saying, "Tell us, when will these things be, and what will be the sign of your coming and of the end of the age?" (Matthew 24:3)

At the time, the disciples did not expect Jesus to leave and then return at some point in the future, so they were not asking about a second coming per se. The disciples asked their question because Jesus had entered Jerusalem the way the prophet Zechariah had said the Messiah would come,[1] but instead of beginning to rule, Jesus gave scathing rebukes to the religious leaders and warned that He would not take His place as King until they welcomed Him.[2] The disciples were completely confused by this series of events. In Matthew 21, it seemed to be the beginning of the fulfillment of what the prophets had said, but then everything changed.

Because the disciples were so perplexed—and understandably so—Jesus quoted several Old Testament passages to demonstrate He remained committed to fulfilling what the Old Testament prophets had predicted. *These prophecies would be fulfilled in a completely unexpected way—namely in two comings rather than one—but they would all be fulfilled.*

We also need to recognize Jesus' progression as a teacher. Matthew 24 is the beginning of His answer to the disciples' question. Matthew 25 is the conclusion of His answer. Like any good teacher, Jesus' answer builds up to a conclusion and an application He expects His audience to respond to. In order to view Jesus' conclusion in context, we need to treat Matthew 24 through 25 as one unit.

Jesus' Use of Old Testament Prophecy

Jesus introduced very little new information in this sermon. He primarily summarized what the prophets had already said. Here are just a few of Jesus' Old Testament references:

- In Matthew 24:15, Jesus referenced Daniel 8:13, 9:27, 12:11, and 11:31 and, therefore, instructed His listeners to study and understand Daniel's prophecy so as to understand His teaching.

- In Matthew 24:21, he quoted Daniel 12:1 directly and in the process also referenced Jeremiah 30:7 and Joel 2:2.

---

[1] See Matthew 21:4–5.

[2] See Matthew 23:39.

- In Matthew 24:22, Jesus alluded to Zechariah 13:8 and 14:2 about the days being cut short.

- In Matthew 24:7, He referenced Zechariah again, specifically Zechariah 9:14, in a simile comparing His coming to lightning.

- In Matthew 24:29, Jesus cited Isaiah 13:9–10 and Joel 2:31 and 3:15. Within the same verse, He also alluded to Isaiah 14:12, Isaiah 34:4, Amos 5:20 and 8:9, and Zephaniah 1:14–15.

- In Matthew 24:30, Jesus quoted Zechariah 12:10–12 and Daniel 7:13–14.

Because Jesus used Old Testament prophecies as the source of His teaching, we must interpret His teaching according to the Old Testament promises. Jesus was not reinterpreting Old Testament expectations; He was affirming them. The process that will fulfill these expectations will be completely different than anyone expected, but the prophecies themselves will come to fruition.

Jesus' Summary of His Return

There is a general flow to Jesus' teaching in these two chapters. He began by summarizing end-time events based on what the prophets had predicted. Jesus affirmed their prophecies and indicated His commitment to fulfill what the prophets had prophesied. Jesus followed this with several parables to illustrate how to live while we are waiting for the fulfillment of these prophecies. After these parables, Jesus gave His conclusion to the entire message in Matthew 25:31–46.

Jesus' conclusion—Matthew 25:31–46—is one of the His most dramatic predictions:

"When the Son of Man comes in his glory, and all the angels with him, then he will sit on his glorious throne. Before him will be gathered all the nations, and he will separate people one from another as a shepherd separates the sheep from the goats. And he will place the sheep on his right, but the goats on the left. Then the King will say to those on his right, 'Come, you who are blessed by my Father, inherit the kingdom prepared for you from the foundation of the world. For I was hungry and you gave me food, I was thirsty and you gave me drink, I was a stranger and you welcomed me, I was naked and you clothed me, I was sick and you visited me, I was in prison and you came to me.' Then the righteous

will answer him, saying, 'Lord, when did we see you hungry and feed you, or thirsty and give you drink? And when did we see you a stranger and welcome you, or naked and clothe you? And when did we see you sick or in prison and visit you?' And the King will answer them, 'Truly, I say to you, as you did it to one of the least of these my brothers, you did it to me.' Then he will say to those on his left, 'Depart from me, you cursed, into the eternal fire prepared for the devil and his angels. For I was hungry and you gave me no food, I was thirsty and you gave me no drink, I was a stranger and you did not welcome me, naked and you did not clothe me, sick and in prison and you did not visit me.' Then they also will answer, saying, 'Lord, when did we see you hungry or thirsty or a stranger or naked or sick or in prison, and did not minister to you?' Then he will answer them, saying, 'Truly, I say to you, as you did not do it to one of the least of these, you did not do it to me.' And these will go away into eternal punishment, but the righteous into eternal life."

Jesus began by identifying Himself as the glorious "Son of Man" from Daniel's vision in Daniel 7.[3] This reference made the section even more dramatic because Daniel 7 described God coming in His glory and putting a "Son of Man" in place to judge the nations:

"I saw in the night visions, and behold, with the clouds of heaven there came one like a son of man, and he came to the Ancient of Days and was presented before him. And to him was given dominion and glory and a kingdom, that all peoples, nations, and languages should serve him; his dominion is an everlasting dominion, which shall not pass away, and his kingdom one that shall not be destroyed." (vv. 13–14)

Considering that this is the dramatic conclusion to Jesus' longest teaching on the end times, we need to give significant attention to it. Different interpretations of the passage through church history have left many believers with the idea that this passage is difficult to understand. In reality, this final section of Jesus' teaching is relatively straightforward.

---

[3] Jesus' use of the phrase *Son of Man* throughout His ministry was very controversial because it is a reference to the exalted Man who judges in the place of God.

Jesus Repeated What the Prophets Predicted

The three keys we identified earlier—taking the sermon as a single unit, recognizing Old Testament references, and noticing Jesus' flow— are what make the sermon's ending relatively easy to understand. Because this passage follows several parables, many people assume this final section is also a parable. However, it is not a parable. It is a literal conclusion to the entire teaching that describes Jesus' judgment of the nations at His return.

Jesus described this judgment because He expected the disciples to remember this part of His teaching and teach the churches to respond to it properly. It is an incredibly serious passage of Scripture that Jesus did not intend to be difficult to understand. This passage is not a new prediction. Jesus repeated a well-known Old Testament prediction in Joel 3:

> *"For behold, in those days and at that time, when I restore the fortunes of Judah and Jerusalem, I will gather all the nations and bring them down to the Valley of Jehoshaphat. And I will enter into judgment with them there, on behalf of my people and my heritage Israel, because they have scattered them among the nations and have divided up my land, and have cast lots for my people, and have traded a boy for a prostitute, and have sold a girl for wine and have drunk it." (vv. 1–3)*

Not only did Jesus reference the language of Joel 3, He also essentially acted out the passage. The Valley of Jehoshaphat[4] is on the east side of Jerusalem. It is what separates the Mount of Olives from the temple mount and the east side of Jerusalem. As He gave this teaching, Jesus sat on the Mount of Olives, looked over the Valley of Jehoshaphat towards the city of Jerusalem, and predicted the day He would gather the nations into this valley just as Joel had predicted.

Jesus Gave a Visual Illustration

As Jesus taught, it is easy to imagine His gesturing with His right hand and His left hand as He described His rewards and His blessings. As Jesus gestured with His left hand, His hand would have pointed to

---

[4] The name *Jehoshaphat* literally means, "YHWH judges," so the phrase *Valley of Jehoshaphat* literally describes it as the place of God's judgment. It is also known as the Kidron Valley.

the Gehenna.[5] Gehenna is a valley to the south of Jerusalem that begins on the southeast corner of the city (remember, Jesus was directly
east of the city on the Mount of Olives). This was Jerusalem's garbage
dump where trash was burned. In Jesus' day, it burned and smoldered
day and night. In English translations of the Bible, every time Jesus
uses the word *hell,* the actual word Jesus used was *Gehenna.* Gehenna
was Jesus' reference point for punishment, and when He predicted He
would cast people to His left hand, His disciples immediately knew
what it meant.

As the disciples listened to Jesus, they were not confused about the
meaning of the passage. Instead, they were shocked by something else.
In Joel 3, YHWH was the One who judged the nations. In Matthew
25:31, Jesus is the One who judges the nations. Jesus' reference to Joel
3 has a powerful revelation: *He is the divine Judge of Joel 3.*[6] As He began
this teaching, the apostles sat shocked, trying to comprehend that the
divine Judge of Joel 3 was sitting in front of them in human flesh.

The Confusing Phrase

What can be confusing in the passage is Jesus' use of the phrase *my
brothers.* Is Jesus referring to the disciples, or is He referring to His
physical brethren, the Jewish people? In a sense, all believers are Jesus'
brothers,[7] so it is certainly a biblical concept that the disciples and all
believers can be considered Jesus' brothers. At the same time, there is a
history in the Old Testament of God identifying with the Jewish people—particularly in their suffering and affliction.[8]

The phrase *my brothers* has to be interpreted based on context, and
in this case the context becomes clear when we look at the key points
in Jesus' judgment:

- The time frame of this passage is Jesus' return. It describes
  Jesus' judgment of the nations at His return.

---

[5] Also known as the Valley of Hinnom.

[6] See also Daniel 7:13–14; Matthew 16:27; 28:18; John 5:22; 17:2; Acts 10:42; 17:31;
Romans 2:16; 2 Corinthians 5:10; 2 Thessalonians 1:7–10; 2 Timothy 4:1; 1 Peter
4:5; Revelation 20:11–12.

[7] See Psalm 89:27; Matthew 12:50; Hebrews 2:10–12; Romans 8:29.

[8] See Deuteronomy 32:10; Isaiah 63:9; Micah 5:3; Zechariah 2:8.

- Jesus is judging the nations based on their practical response to His brothers.

- Jesus rewards those who were willing to serve His brothers in crisis.

- Jesus refers to His brothers as the *least of these.*

When we look at Joel 3, the basis of God's evaluation is plain, and it explains why the disciples were not confused about the meaning of this passage:

> *"I will gather all the nations and bring them down to the Valley of Jehoshaphat. And I will enter into judgment with them there, on behalf of my people and my heritage Israel, because they have scattered them among the nations and have divided up my land, and have cast lots for my people, and have traded a boy for a prostitute, and have sold a girl for wine and have drunk it." (vv. 2–3)*

Joel predicted a time would come when God judged the nations on behalf of His people and His heritage—Israel. Joel's description of what preceded that judgment makes sense of the phrase *least of these.* The nations will turn against the Jewish people in an unparalleled way, seeking to oppress, marginalize, and even eliminate them. We have summarized the coming rage against Israel, and it makes sense of Joel's prediction that God will gather the nations into the Valley of Jehoshaphat—which He refers to as the *valley of decision*—and release His wrath on them:

> *Proclaim this among the nations: Consecrate for war; stir up the mighty men. Let all the men of war draw near; let them come up. Beat your plowshares into swords, and your pruning hooks into spears; let the weak say, "I am a warrior." Hasten and come, all you surrounding nations, and gather yourselves there. Bring down your warriors, O Lord. Let the nations stir themselves up and come up to the Valley of Jehoshaphat; for there I will sit to judge all the surrounding nations. Put in the sickle, for the harvest is ripe. Go in, tread, for the winepress is full. The vats overflow, for their evil is great. Multitudes, multitudes, in the valley of decision! For the day of the Lord is near in the valley of decision. (Joel 3:9–14)*

A Consistent Prediction

Joel 3 is not an isolated prediction. It is consistent with other passages that predict a day will come that begins with the nations raging against Israel and ends with God's sudden and dramatic judgment of the nations on Israel's behalf.

Zechariah predicted the same event:

> *"Behold, I am going to make Jerusalem a cup that causes reeling to all the peoples around; and when the siege is against Jerusalem, it will also be against Judah. "It will come about in that day that I will make Jerusalem a heavy stone for all the peoples; all who lift it will be severely injured. And all the nations of the earth will be gathered against it. "In that day," declares the Lord, "I will strike every horse with bewilderment and his rider with madness. But I will watch over the house of Judah, while I strike every horse of the peoples with blindness. (Zechariah 12:2–4 NASB)*

> *Behold, a day is coming for the Lord when the spoil taken from you will be divided among you. For I will gather all the nations against Jerusalem to battle, and the city will be captured, the houses plundered, the women ravished and half of the city exiled, but the rest of the people will not be cut off from the city. Then the Lord will go forth and fight against those nations, as when He fights on a day of battle. In that day His feet will stand on the Mount of Olives, which is in front of Jerusalem on the east; and the Mount of Olives will be split in its middle from east to west by a very large valley, so that half of the mountain will move toward the north and the other half toward the south. You will flee by the valley of My mountains, for the valley of the mountains will reach to Azel; yes, you will flee just as you fled before the earthquake in the days of Uzziah king of Judah. Then the Lord, my God, will come, and all the holy ones with Him! . . . And the LORD will be king over all the earth; in that day the Lord will be the only one, and His name the only one. (14:1–5, 9 NASB)*

Isaiah also predicted the same event with even stronger language:

> *The sound of a tumult is on the mountains as of a great multitude! The sound of an uproar of kingdoms, of nations gathering together! The Lord of hosts is mustering a host for battle. They come from a distant*

land, from the end of the heavens, the Lord and the weapons of his indignation, to destroy the whole land. Wail, for the day of the Lord is near; as destruction from the Almighty it will come! (Isaiah 13:4–6)

Draw near, O nations, to hear, and give attention, O peoples! Let the earth hear, and all that fills it; the world, and all that comes from it. For the Lord is enraged against all the nations, and furious against all their host; he has devoted them to destruction, has given them over for slaughter. Their slain shall be cast out, and the stench of their corpses shall rise; the mountains shall flow with their blood. . . . For the Lord has a day of vengeance, a year of recompense for the cause of Zion. (34:1–3, 8)

Zephaniah also used vivid language about this day:

The great day of the Lord is near, near and hastening fast; the sound of the day of the Lord is bitter; the mighty man cries aloud there. A day of wrath is that day, a day of distress and anguish, a day of ruin and devastation, a day of darkness and gloom, a day of clouds and thick darkness. (Zephaniah 1:14–15)

"Therefore wait for me," declares the Lord, "for the day when I rise up to seize the prey. For my decision is to gather nations, to assemble kingdoms, to pour out upon them my indignation, all my burning anger; for in the fire of my jealousy all the earth shall be consumed." . . . Sing aloud, O daughter of Zion; shout, O Israel! Rejoice and exult with all your heart, O daughter of Jerusalem! The Lord has taken away the judgments against you; he has cleared away your enemies. The King of Israel, the Lord, is in your midst; you shall never again fear evil. . . . "The Lord your God is in your midst, a mighty one who will save; he will rejoice over you with gladness; he will quiet you by his love; he will exult over you with loud singing. . . . Behold, at that time I will deal with all your oppressors. And I will save the lame and gather the outcast, and I will change their shame into praise and renown in all the earth. At that time I will bring you in, at the time when I gather you together; for I will make you renowned and praised among all the peoples of the earth, when I restore your fortunes before your eyes," says the Lord. (3:8, 14–15, 17, 19–20)

This event is summarized repeatedly throughout the prophets,[9] and these prophecies have never been fulfilled. Jerusalem has endured multiple invasions but never an invasion of a multitude of nations that is interrupted by God releasing His wrath on the invading nations. All the ancient sieges on Jerusalem have ended with Israel's suffering at the hands of the nations, but the prophets predict a siege that ends in Israel's salvation and the nations being judged by God based on their treatment of her. *This is the event Matthew 25 refers to.*

Jesus is not referring to the judgment of the saints. They are gathered to Jesus as soon as He appears before He comes to Jerusalem.[10] This is not the judgment of every individual in history. This is an event that will occur at Jesus' return. On that day, Jesus will be able to judge the nations based on their response to Jerusalem because the end-time conflict that will erupt around Israel will be an expression of rage against Jesus.

The Implications of Jesus' End-Time Judgment

Jesus' prediction of His judgment as His return was consistent with what the prophets had predicted. Because this is Jesus' conclusion to His longest teaching on the end times, He expects us to wrestle with the profound implications it has for the church and the nations.

When we consider Matthew 25 carefully and soberly, in light of all the Bible says about Jesus' return and His judgment of the nations, we are left with a staggering prediction: *Before the return of Jesus, the dynamics on the earth are going to shift in such a way that Jesus can evaluate the nations based on one question: How did they respond to the people of Israel in the midst of an end-time crisis?*

This will not be the only issue in the end times. The Bible describes many other signs that will be prominent in the end. However, the unique dynamics that will emerge around Israel will make it a litmus test that Jesus can use for His judgment. We saw a small example of this in the Nazi Holocaust, but the end-time conflict over Israel's future will be much more intense. *Jesus' end-time judgment of the nations reveals God will hold the nations accountable to His covenant with Israel.* As we will see,

---

[9] See also Jeremiah 30:7–11; Daniel 12:1.

[10] See 1 Corinthians 15:23, 52; 1 Thessalonians 4:16–17.

the nations will be given a witness of that covenant through both the Scripture and the witness given by the church.

The prediction that Jesus can judge the nations based on their response to the Jewish people during the rage of the Antichrist is simply staggering. It reveals three things about the coming crisis:

- It indicates the magnitude of the end-time crisis. Something is coming that is far beyond anything we can imagine.

- The church must understand what the Bible says about the crisis and Jesus' judgment of the nations. These verses were given to us so that we can prepare the church and the nations for what is coming before it happens.[11]

- The coming crisis around Israel will be directly connected to the earth's controversy with Jesus, justifying God's judging the nations. The ultimate conflict in the earth is not over Israel; it is over Jesus. We must understand this connection so we can give a clear witness to the nations.

None of the previous conflicts over Israel have ever triggered God's judgment of the nations. Something far beyond what we can imagine is coming—something that will justify the release of God's end-time judgments. There are two challenges we face that can keep us from fully appreciating the magnitude of what is coming. One challenge is to assume this is all exaggerated language. However, when we look closely, none of these predictions were fulfilled in ancient history. When we consider the intricate details of prophecy that were fulfilled in Jesus' first coming, it should alert us to take passages referring to His second coming very seriously.

The other challenge is to not fully grasp the magnitude of previous conflicts over Jerusalem. We tend to quickly read over accounts of the Babylonian invasion of Jerusalem or the fall of Jerusalem in AD 70 with very little emotion and little consideration of what those events really involved. Jeremiah tells us that the Babylonian siege was so horrific mothers were willing to eat their children. According to Josephus,

---

[11] The is part of the testimony or witness "of the kingdom" required to fulfill Matthew 24:14.

the Romans killed over a million people[12] when they laid siege to Jerusalem in the first century and ran out of trees to use for crosses because they crucified so many people.[13] The tragedy was so immense the Roman conqueror Titus is reported to have refused a victory-wreath, saying there was "no merit in vanquishing people forsaken by their own God."[14]

We are so far removed from what actually happened in the ancient world that it hardly seems real to us. However, to understand what the prophets are trying to tell us, we must soberly understand what has happened in the past. When we really feel the weight of history, the predictions the prophets made become far more vivid and ominous. If the Bible is to be taken literally, and the first coming of Jesus shows it should be, there are days ahead of us that we are completely unprepared for.

Some scholars treat the passionate language of the prophets as though it is simply hyperbolic language describing a mostly spiritual conflict. However, their language is not merely hyperbolic. It is the language of men incapacitated by the predictions they were given of the final moments of this age when both righteousness and wickedness reach maturity and come into an unprecedented conflict. *God intends we take their words seriously.*

Responding to Jesus' Words

The Bible does not say the nations in every generation are judged according to their understanding of God's plans and purposes for Israel, but the Bible does predict that a moment will come, just before the return of the Lord, when the Lord will require the nations to agree with His purposes for Israel or face His wrath. However, most of the church does not understand this is coming, and very few are preparing the church for this crisis.

These predictions were given to us for two reasons:

1. To give us hope and courage about the future by understanding God's victory and the end of Satan's resistance.

---

[12] Josephus, *The Wars of the Jews*, 6:420.

[13] Josephus, *The Wars of the Jews*, 5:449–41.

[14] Philostratus, *The Life of Apollonius of Tyana*, 6.29.

2. To make us aware of what is coming so that we can partner with God in His mission as a people with understanding.

We must study what the Scripture says about the coming crisis so we instruct our children, our churches, and even our nations. When Jesus predicted He would judge the nations according to their response to Israel's end-time crisis, He was not saying that Israel would become the final issue in the earth. He was saying that Israel, in the last generation, will become a litmus test that can be used to evaluate nations. This means the crisis over Israel's salvation will become so severe it will be a reliable measure of the nations' response to Israel's Messiah.

When the nations gather for their final siege on Jerusalem, it will be a visible expression of their rage against the heavenly Jerusalem and the King who dwells in that city. It will be an ultimate expression of hatred for the God of Israel, His chosen method of salvation, and His chosen King. *We must be able to communicate to others why a crisis that seems to be centered on Israel is actually centered on the King of Jerusalem.*

THE MISSION BEFORE THE END

Throughout the Bible, God instructed nations before He released His judgments. Before the flood, Noah was sent as a preacher.[1] Before God brought Israel out of Egypt, He sent Moses to warn Pharaoh. Moses made it clear to Pharaoh what God wanted, and Pharaoh was challenged to respond. Though Pharaoh refused God's warning and suffered God's judgments, the warning, nonetheless, was given. Before God's judgments came on Israel, He sent prophets. God even warned pagan nations. Assyria was a wicked, gentile nation, but God sent Jonah to call it to repentance before God's judgments fell.

Regardless of whether people and nations respond, God is faithful to give a witness before He releases His judgments. The New Testament apostles saw the preaching of the gospel and the Great Commission as a continuation of this pattern. Therefore, they did more than evangelize; they spoke of God's end-time judgments and called the people to repentance.

New Testament Missions in Light of the End Times

By considering a few passages, we can quickly see how the New Testament apostles functioned in a way that was similar to the Old Testament prophets.

The apostles warned the nations of the coming end-time judgments and the return of the Jesus:

"And he commanded us to preach to the people and to testify that he is the one appointed by God to be judge of the living and the dead." (Acts 10:42)

---

[1] See 2 Peter 2:5.

"The times of ignorance God overlooked, but now he commands all people everywhere to repent, because he has fixed a day on which he will judge the world in righteousness by a man whom he has appointed; and of this he has given assurance to all by raising him from the dead." (17:30–31)

But because of your stubbornness and unrepentant heart you are storing up wrath for yourself in the day of wrath and revelation of the righteous judgment of God, who WILL RENDER TO EACH PERSON ACCORDING TO HIS DEEDS. (Romans 2:5–6 NASB)

But they will give account to Him who is ready to judge the living and the dead. (1 Peter 4:5 NASB)

The end of all things is near; therefore, be of sound judgment and sober spirit for the purpose of prayer. (v. 7 NASB)

But by the same word the heavens and earth that now exist are stored up for fire, being kept until the day of judgment and destruction of the ungodly. (2 Peter 3:7)

It was also about these that Enoch, the seventh from Adam, prophesied, saying, "Behold, the Lord comes with ten thousands of his holy ones, to execute judgment on all and to convict all the ungodly of all their deeds of ungodliness that they have committed in such an ungodly way, and of all the harsh things that ungodly sinners have spoken against him." (Jude 14–15)

The apostles prepared the church to face God's judgments:

On the day when, according to my gospel, God will judge the secrets of men through Christ Jesus. (Romans 2:16 NASB)

For to this end Christ died and lived again, that He might be Lord both of the dead and of the living. But you, why do you judge your brother? Or you again, why do you regard your brother with contempt? For we will all stand before the judgment seat of God. (Romans 14:9–10 NASB)

Now if anyone builds on the foundation with gold, silver, precious stones, wood, hay, straw—each one's work will become manifest, for the Day will disclose it, because it will be revealed by fire, and the fire will test what sort of work each one has done. (1 Corinthians 3:12–13)

For we must all appear before the judgment seat of Christ, so that each one may receive what is due for what he has done in the body, whether good or evil. (2 Corinthians 5:10)

In the future there is laid up for me the crown of righteousness, which the Lord, the righteous Judge, will award to me on that day; and not only to me, but also to all who have loved His appearing. (2 Timothy 4:8 NASB)

Then the Lord knows how to rescue the godly from trials, and to keep the unrighteous under punishment until the day of judgment. (2 Peter 2:9)

By this, love is perfected with us, so that we may have confidence in the day of judgment; because as He is, so also are we in this world. (1 John 4:17 NASB)

Paul's ministry in Thessalonica is a good example of how the apostles communicated the gospel. In Thessalonica, Paul was accused of declaring another King who was superior to Caesar:

And when they could not find them, they dragged Jason and some of the brothers before the city authorities, shouting, "These men who have turned the world upside down have come here also, and Jason has received them, and they are all acting against the decrees of Caesar, saying that there is another king, Jesus." And the people and the city authorities were disturbed when they heard these things. (Acts 17:6–8)

The city authorities were disturbed because Paul's preaching went beyond private religious practice. Paul preached Jesus as a King coming with His judgments and warned the nations to repent and submit to Jesus before He came with His judgments. Paul's teaching in the churches was very similar. Paul was only in Thessalonica for a short period of time, but he taught this new church plant in-depth information about the return of Jesus:

For you yourselves are fully aware that the day of the Lord will come like a thief in the night. . . . But you are not in darkness, brothers, for that day to surprise you like a thief. For you are all children of light, children of the day. We are not of the night or of the darkness. So then let us not sleep, as others do, but let us keep awake and be sober. (1 Thessalonians 5:2, 4–6)

196 It Must Be Finished

Paul placed a priority on warning the nations and preparing the church for Jesus' end-time judgments. Paul simultaneously warned the nations *and* prepared the churches for the coming of Jesus. Paul saw this as part of the missionary call.

First John reveals the apostles taught on the return of Jesus and some of the details that surround His return:

Children, it is the last hour, and as you have heard that antichrist is coming, so now many antichrists have come. Therefore we know that it is the last hour. (2:18)

By this you know the Spirit of God: every spirit that confesses that Jesus Christ has come in the flesh is from God, and every spirit that does not confess Jesus is not from God. This is the spirit of the antichrist, which you heard was coming and now is in the world already. (4:2–3)

John reminded the people they had been taught about the coming Antichrist. This reveals the apostles valued teaching about the return of Jesus enough to give the church insight and understanding about what was coming. John also connected their teaching about the coming Antichrist to the "many antichrists" on the earth right now. John reminded the church that the end-time crisis is similar in nature to the trials the church faces throughout history.

Though the end is unique in its magnitude, there will be many antichrists and periods of tribulation throughout history. We may or may not live through the reign of the Antichrist, but it is likely we will live through the rule of at least one antichrist figure. *This is one of the keys to teaching the end times correctly. When we prepare the church for the end-time crisis, we are also preparing the church to properly respond to the crises in our generation, even if we do not live through the end-time crisis.*

Living in the Light of Jesus' Return

While the first-century church did not live to see the return of Jesus, they lived in light of it. Their expectation of Jesus' return and preparation for it served the church well. It enabled the church to take root in a hostile environment and endure periods of suffering.

Paul continued to lay this foundation his entire ministry. In 2 Timothy, likely Paul's final letter, Paul gave Timothy specific instructions:

I charge you in the presence of God and of Christ Jesus, who is to judge the living and the dead, and by his appearing and his kingdom: preach the word; be ready in season and out of season; reprove, rebuke, and exhort, with complete patience and teaching. For the time is coming when people will not endure sound teaching, but having itching ears they will accumulate for themselves teachers to suit their own passions, and will turn away from listening to the truth and wander off into myths. As for you, always be sober-minded, endure suffering, do the work of an evangelist, fulfill your ministry. (4:1–5)

Paul charged Timothy to preach in light of Jesus' return and the accompanying judgments. The phrase *the living and the dead* was used by early Christians to describe Jesus' judgments at His return.[2] George Knight summarizes Paul's motivation well:

Just as the thought of the judgment by Christ of all people motivated Paul, so Paul wanted it to motivate Timothy.[3]

Paul warned Timothy more challenging times were coming, and this was why he must stay faithful in his assignment. We can summarize verses 1 through 4 this way: *In light of the Lord's coming judgments and the deception that will fill the earth, faithfully prepare the people for what is coming.* Paul gave Timothy a vision for pastoral ministry that included preparing the people for end-time events. Paul exhorted Timothy to be steadfast and faithful in this ministry regardless of the seasons he passed through.

Paul commanded Timothy in verse 5 to "do the work of an evangelist." We define evangelism as speaking the gospel to unbelievers so they make a confession of faith and experience the new birth. However, we cannot take this modern definition and assume Paul used the term in the exact same way we do. Paul's understanding of evangelism—proclaiming the good news—included the entire charge he gave Timothy.

---

[2] Thomas D. Lea and Hayne P. Griffin, *1, 2 Timothy, Titus*, vol. 34, The New American Commentary (Nashville: Broadman & Holman Publishers, 1992), 242.

[3] George W. Knight, *The Pastoral Epistles: A Commentary on the Greek Text*, New International Greek Testament Commentary (Grand Rapids, MI; Carlisle, England: W.B. Eerdmans; Paternoster Press, 1992), 452.

The Great Commission Is More than Evangelism

Paul understood evangelism as more than a conversion. It included proclaiming the gospel so that some people experienced conversion, but it also included warning people of the coming judgment and preparing the church for Jesus' return and the unique dynamics that surround His return. This does not minimize the ministry of evangelism that brings individuals to the point of conversion. It simply means Paul saw the preparation of people for the return of the Lord as part of the work of evangelism.

Paul understood the Great Commission was more than evangelism. It was a command to disciple the nations to obey everything Jesus taught:

> *And Jesus came up and spoke to them, saying, "All authority has been given to Me in heaven and on earth. Go therefore and make disciples of all the nations, baptizing them in the name of the Father and the Son and the Holy Spirit, teaching them to observe all that I commanded you; and lo, I am with you always, even to the end of the age." (Matthew 28:18–20 NASB)*

We tend to reduce the Great Commission to evangelism, but Jesus commanded us to go into the nations and disciple people to "observe *all*" that He had commanded. This explains why passages like Matthew 24 through 25 are so critical. They are part of what Jesus commanded, and we must disciple the nations to obey these passages.

Furthermore, because Jesus is the divine Word of God,[4] all Scripture can be considered His words. Therefore, the command to disciple the nations to obey everything Jesus taught includes teaching nations to study and obey all that He has said in the Scripture. This includes passages like Joel 3 and many others that describe the coming judgment and the events that surround the return of Jesus.

Missions Is More than Evangelism

In our generation, the church is mobilizing laborers to finish the task of evangelizing every tribe and tongue. This is extremely important, but the evangelization of the nations is only one step of missions. To fulfill the task Jesus gave, we must also disciple the nations to obey

---

[4] See John 1:1; Revelation 19:10.

all that Jesus has commanded. *The Holocaust is a shocking warning of what can happen to an unprepared church and an unprepared nation when they have not been discipled to obey all Jesus commanded.* In light of what the Scripture says, we cannot afford to be unprepared for the final crisis.

Some have made preparing for the return of the Lord primarily about trying to figure out the date of Jesus' return or predicting the identity of the Antichrist, but that is not what the first-century church did. When you read the New Testament, there is a strong emphasis on the return of Jesus, but the writers never interpreted Roman politics according to their end-time expectations. They simply proclaimed what the Bible said and lived according to it.

Preparing the church for the Lord's return is not primarily about interpreting political events; it is primarily about the maturity of the church. Preparing the church for the return of the Lord in a biblical way strengthens the church to resist the Antichrist who is coming and also the many antichrists who are already in the earth.[5] This is part of the work of missions.

When we survey the ministry of the church in the New Testament, we are left with a profound conclusion: Missions is more than evangelism.

When we think of preparing people for the return of the Lord, we think primarily of discipling people to live in holiness and personal devotion. This is incredibly important, but it is only the beginning of preparing people for the return of the Lord. The apostles studied what the Scripture says about unique dynamics that accompany the return of the Lord, they taught it boldly, and they prepared the people for that great day.

We must understand and teach the main biblical themes of the return of the Lord so the church is prepared and the nations are warned to repent before the great and terrible day comes. When we speak about judgment, we tend to speak about it in general terms, but Scripture gives us many specific details about the coming judgments. We are called to study and know these details.

---

[5] See 1 John 2:18

Missions Exists to Prepare the Nations for Jesus' Return

Matthew 24:14 has become a rally cry to missions for many in the church:

"And this gospel of the kingdom will be proclaimed throughout the whole world as a testimony to all nations, and then the end will come."

This verse is one of the foundations of modern missions, but we must view it in context to understand everything that is implicated in the verse. This verse is in a larger context—Matthew 24 through 25—that we examined in the previous chapter. That context must influence our understanding of what it takes to fulfill the verse. We have also seen that the early church interpreted the missions as an assignment to prepare the nations for the return of Jesus. That paradigm must also affect how we view Matthew 24:14.

The activity of the early church demonstrated information about Jesus' return should have a missional application because Jesus wants us to prepare the nations for His judgments. The overall structure of Jesus' sermon in Matthew 24 through 25 emphasizes the missional nature of the sermon. Here is the structure of the sermon from a missional perspective:

- Matthew 24:4–14—Jesus' introduction.
- Matthew 24:15–35—key events of the end times.
- Matthew 24:36–25:30—instructions and parables on how to prepare for end-time events.
- Matthew 25:31–46—Jesus' end-time judgment of the nations.

In His introduction, Jesus gave specific signs of the times the church would face throughout history. These signs will escalate as we enter the end times. This section teaches that preparation is valuable in every generation because each generation will face a measure of the challenges of the end of the age. This is what the apostle John meant when he said there were "many antichrists."[6]

Jesus concluded His introduction with Matthew 24:14 and a prediction the end of the age would not come until a testimony was given

---

[6] See 1 John 2:18.

throughout the earth of the gospel of the kingdom. The gospel of the kingdom is an end-time statement. When we speak of Jesus as King, we are not just saying Jesus is a spiritual leader. We are saying He is the rightful Ruler of the earth who is coming to sit on a real throne in Jerusalem, fulfill all God has promised, and destroy everything opposed to God's purposes.

Not only is the gospel of Jesus as King to be proclaimed, it is also to be proclaimed as a witness, which is a reference to the function of an ancient herald. An ancient herald would enter a city before a king came to announce the king was coming and to prepare the city for that king. The disciples understood what Jesus was saying. The church must become His "herald" to every nation, announcing His coming and instructing the earth to prepare for His coming. This was the work of an ancient herald, and Jesus has commissioned His people to perform that function on His behalf. (Paul described apostles as "ambassadors" for similar reasons.[7])

To fulfill Matthew 24:14, we must prepare the nations for Jesus' prediction in Matthew 24:15:

> *So when you see the abomination of desolation spoken of by the prophet Daniel, standing in the holy place (let the reader understand).* . . .

This verse begins with *therefore* in some translations[8] and *so* in others. The word *so* or *therefore* is a connecting word that makes Matthew 24:15 the result of Matthew 24:14. To say it another way, Matthew 24:14 prepares the earth for Matthew 24:15 and the events that follow. This verse is a statement of God's great kindness. *He will not allow the Antichrist to emerge and the end-time drama to begin until the nations are prepared by a witness given by the church.*

The first-century church understood this. They prepared the church for Jesus' return and warned the nations that Jesus was coming with His judgments. We need to understand the main themes of Jesus' overview of end-time events in Matthew 24:15–35 and His judgment of the nations in Mathew 25:31–46, because part of the task of mis-

---

[7] See 2 Corinthians 5:20; Ephesians 6:20.

[8] The New American Standard and New King James Version are two examples.

sions is preparing nations for these events. *God is too kind to allow the events of the end times to begin before the nations are warned and prepared.*

This is one of the reasons Jesus' end-time judgments are so severe. Before the end times begin, the church will give the nations a powerful warning of what is coming. Just as Moses made clear to Pharaoh what God's demands were before God released His judgments on Egypt, the church will declare the beauty of Jesus and His coming judgments in such a way that the nations will have no excuse at His return. The end-time rage of the nations is not merely a manifestation of sin; it is a complete rejection of the gospel of the kingdom which will have been declared in all the nations.

Paul's Concern for the Gentile Churches

Paul's ministry demonstrates he labored to prepare the gentile churches for Jesus' judgment (Matthew 25:31–46) by connecting the gentile churches to Jerusalem in a practical way. Before his first missionary journey, Paul traveled from Antioch to Jerusalem to deliver a financial gift from a predominantly gentile church to the believers in Judea:

> *So the disciples determined, every one according to his ability, to send relief to the brothers living in Judea. (Acts 11:29)*

In his letter to the Galatians, Paul described his gladness at calling the gentile churches to donate to the believers in Jerusalem:

> *And when James and Cephas and John, who seemed to be pillars, perceived the grace that was given to me, they gave the right hand of fellowship to Barnabas and me, that we should go to the Gentiles and they to the circumcised. Only, they asked us to remember the poor, the very thing I was eager to do. (Galatians 2:9–10)*

Paul was asked to "remember the poor," and this phrase is shorthand for remembering the poor in Jerusalem.[9] When the apostles asked Paul to remember them, the apostles in Jerusalem were not demanding support from the gentile churches. The apostles wanted to see a deep friendship between Jewish and gentile believers. They heard Jesus deliv-

---

[9] Timothy George, vol. 30, *Galatians, The New American Commentary* (Nashville: Broadman & Holman Publishers, 1994), 165.

er the teaching of Matthew 25, and they knew how critical it was that the Gentiles stay connected to the Jewish people in a practical way. These small practical steps were designed to do just that so the church would be prepared for the end-time crisis.

In 1 Corinthians, Paul also encouraged the church in Corinth to give to the church in Jerusalem:

> *Now concerning the collection for the saints: as I directed the churches of Galatia, so you also are to do. On the first day of every week, each of you is to put something aside and store it up, as he may prosper, so that there will be no collecting when I come. And when I arrive, I will send those whom you accredit by letter to carry your gift to Jerusalem. (16:1–3)*

Paul spoke at length about this collection in 2 Corinthians 8 through 9 and addressed this issue in his letter to the Romans. Paul also gave a masterful teaching in Romans 9 through 11 strongly warning the gentile church not to become arrogant:

> *But if some of the branches were broken off, and you, although a wild olive shoot, were grafted in among the others and now share in the nourishing root of the olive tree, do not be arrogant toward the branches. If you are, remember it is not you who support the root, but the root that supports you. (Romans 11:17–18)*

Paul knew Israel's failure to respond to the gospel could easily result in gentile believers becoming arrogant towards Israel and her unbelief. He knew an arrogant gentile church would be easily deceived by the enemy and turned from her purpose to minister to the Jewish people. *Tragically, church history has validated Paul's concerns.* Therefore, Paul encouraged the church in Rome to practically sow into the Jewish people:

> *For Macedonia and Achaia have been pleased to make some contribution for the poor among the saints at Jerusalem. For they were pleased to do it, and indeed they owe it to them. For if the Gentiles have come to share in their spiritual blessings, they ought also to be of service to them in material blessings. (Romans 15:26–27)*

The fact that Paul addressed this in multiple letters to multiples cities shows how significant the collection for the saints in Jerusalem was to him. He did not demand a collection from the Gentiles because it was some sort of spiritual tax for the mother church. He called for a free will offering given out of love and affection. Paul had a genuine concern for the needs of the church in Jerusalem, but this collection was more than a response to a temporary need.

Part of Paul's emphasis on practically serving the church in Jerusalem came from Paul's understanding of the end-time crisis. He understood part of his work was to prepare Gentiles to love and serve Israel. He knew that Israel would become a litmus test for the nations in the last days, and he was laboring among the Gentiles to keep their hearts tender and connected to Israel in practical ways so that the Gentiles would be prepared when the hour came. Paul prioritized support for the believers in Jerusalem, indicating that the most important relationship between the Gentiles and Israel was the relationship between gentile and Jewish believers.

Preparing the Gentile Church

Paul shared a deep anguish over Israel's salvation[10] and called the Gentiles to share his burden.[11] In his commentary on Galatians, Timothy George makes the following observation:

> *J. Munck, among others, has interpreted the Pauline collection in terms of the apostle's eschatological hope for the conversion of Israel. It has been suggested that Paul may have hoped that his deliverance of a large collection from the Gentile churches would lead to the mass conversion of many Jews in Jerusalem thus preparing the way for the dawn of the messianic age.[12]*

As we get near the end of the book of Acts, we find that Israel's salvation remained deep in Paul's heart:

> *"It is because of the hope of Israel that I am wearing this chain." (28:20)*

---

[10] See Romans 9:2; 10:1.

[11] See Romans 11.

[12] Timothy George, vol. 30, *Galatians, The New American Commentary* (Nashville: Broadman & Holman Publishers, 1994), 165.

The first-century church understood gentile responsibility to serve the Jew and took it very seriously. Their Israel-centric paradigm, which saw the gentile church not as a completely new entity but as the inclusion of the nations into God's purposes for Israel, made gentile ministry to the Jew a priority. Their concern for the gentile churches shows us Jesus' warning in Matthew 25:31–46 was taken literally by the apostles. They understood and communicated gentile responsibility for Israel. Given the apostles' proximity to Jesus, their actions are significant to how the first-century church understood Matthew 24 through 25.

The apostles emphasized practical responses because Jesus' judgment of the nations will evaluate practical responses. In the same way, we need to not only disciple the nations into the right beliefs, we must also instruct them in the right behavior. This is why passages like Matthew 24 through 25 are not optional. They must shape and affect how we do missions and how we disciple nations. The end of the age is not only going to test what people believe; it is going to test what people do because that is the ultimate measure of what they believe.

We have seen how the Bible predicts that Jerusalem, Israel's salvation, and Israel's King will become a global controversy that will touch all the nations. *This is especially important for us because we now live in the first generation in human history where the issue of Israel has become a global controversy.* This has never happened before in history.

Christians tend to recognize the significant role Israel has played throughout redemptive history because of the way the Bible focuses on her story. However, in the ancient world, the vast majority of the earth had no interest in what was happening in the Middle East. The most dramatic events of the Bible were all regional events that had very little impact outside of the immediate region. The world we live in is dramatically different. The issue of Israel and Jerusalem has now become a global issue. Every continent is involved. Nations thousands of miles away have interest in Jerusalem and bold opinions about what should be done with that city.

There is no natural reason for this focus. Jerusalem is not the center of a great oil reserve. It is not an international center of banking or a hub of global commerce. While God has blessed that region in many ways, there is simply no logical reason why Jerusalem and Israel should be a global issue. Some say it is due to the humanitarian situation related to the Palestinians—and that is worthy of attention—but there are much larger humanitarian crises in the earth that are nearly ignored. The geopolitical realities simply do not justify the myopic focus of the nations on Jerusalem.

The United Nations is just one example. In 2016, the UN adopted twenty resolutions against Israel and only six on the rest of the earth.[13] Nor is this unusual. In 2015, the UN adopted twenty resolutions against Israel and only three on the rest of the earth.[14] When we consider the geopolitical events of 2015 and 2016, it is simply unbelievable the earth's global leaders saw fit to spend exponentially more time on the issue of Israel than other calamities affecting millions more people.

We are currently facing the largest humanitarian crisis since World War II with more than twenty million people at risk of starvation.[15] Dictators and would-be-dictators around the earth are flexing their muscles and, in some cases, annexing territory from other nations. Entire nations have disintegrated. Radical Islamic terrorism has unleashed incredible carnage. There are millions of refugees in the earth. In the midst of all these crises that are challenging dozens of nations, the UN singles out Israel as the issue most needing to be addressed. This simply has no rational explanation outside of what the Bible says will happen.

The Bible predicts that the Middle East will become the center of the world events in the end times. The global story is going to return to the place where it began. In our generation, the Middle East is beginning to affect the earth in a way that it never has. Economics are affected by the Middle East due to the oil economy. Radical Islam has transformed from a regional religion to a global challenge. The Middle East refugee crisis is disrupting nations and challenging the globe. We

---

[13] UN Watch. "UNGA Adopts 20 Resolutions Against Israel, 6 on Rest of World Combined." Last modified December 21, 2016. Accessed March 24, 2017. https://www.unwatch.org/unga-adopts-20-resolutions-israel-4-rest-world-combined/.

[14] UN Watch. "UN adopts 20 Resolutions Against Israel, 3 on Rest of the World." Last modified November 25, 2015. Accessed March 24, 2017. https://www.unwatch.org/un-to-adopt-20-resolutions-against-israel-3-on-rest-of-the-world/.

[15] *The Two-Way Breaking News from NPR.* "World Faces Largest Humanitarian Crisis Since 1945, U.N. Official Says." Last modified March 11, 2017. Accessed March 24, 2017. http://www.npr.org/sections/thetwo-way/2017/03/11/519832515/world-faces-largest-humanitarian-crisis-since-1945-u-n-official-says.

have to recognize what is happening. Slowly the stage is being set for a drama in the Middle East that will capture the entire world just as the Bible predicts.

This growing storm simply does not make sense apart from spiritual realities. There is something much greater going on than what we see in our newspaper headlines. The geopolitical events now unfolding are indicators of a bigger story, and the Bible tells us where that story is going and how it will be resolved.

While we do not know when the events the Bible predicts will happen, we must be sober that we now live in the first time in human history when these events are possible. That means we must understand what the Bible says, labor for a mature church that can be faithful in the middle of an end-time crisis, and warn the nations to respond to the gospel.

The Holocaust seemed to seize the nations suddenly. However, the end-time crisis is brewing in the nations, and we have been given time to prepare. It is unwise to try to time that crisis. It may be with us for a long time, or it may escalate quickly. It is wise, though, to recognize we now live in the first generation in human history where the things prophesied about the end-time crisis are possible. That must affect how we study the Bible, how we pastor the church, and how we do missions.

HOW TO RESPOND TO PROPHECY

God has given us a tremendous amount of information about how He will fulfill His promises. He gave us this information because He loves partnering with His people. He will work closely with and through His people to prepare the earth for the return of Jesus. These predictions give us a roadmap for world missions. In the same way that understanding the destination helps us plan a trip, by knowing where the redemptive story is going, we can better partner with God in His purposes for the earth.

For example, when we read Matthew 24:14, Matthew 28:19, Revelation 5:9, and Revelation 7:9, we discover God wants the gospel preached to every people group:

"This gospel of the kingdom shall be preached in the whole world as a testimony to all the nations, and then the end will come." (Matthew 24:14 NASB)

"Go therefore and make disciples of all the nations, baptizing them in the name of the Father and the Son and the Holy Spirit. . . ." (28:19 NASB)

And they sang a new song, saying, "Worthy are You to take the book and to break its seals; for You were slain, and purchased for God with Your blood men from every tribe and tongue and people and nation." (Revelation 5:9 NASB)

After these things I looked, and behold, a great multitude which no one could count, from every nation and all tribes and peoples and tongues, standing before the throne and before the Lamb, clothed in white robes, and palm branches were in their hands. (7:9 NASB)

210 It Must Be Finished

Only God can fulfill prophecy, but within prophecy we find descriptions of the end-time church and insight for missions. She will be a church of every tribe and tongue. She will be a unified and mature church. She will be a church that agrees with God's purposes for Israel. She will express herself in extravagant prayer and worship. All these descriptions of the end-time church are given to us so that we can labor with God to see the church come to this level of maturity.

We are used to reading prophecy only as information, but prophecy is truly an invitation. It calls us to participate in God's mission. It contains instructions for the church. We have recognized this in passages like Matthew 24:14, Revelation 5:9, and Revelation 7:9, but we need to begin to read all Bible prophecy the way we read these verses.

Be Prepared in Every Generation

The Bible instructs the church to be prepared for the return of Jesus in every generation. The apostles warned us that many antichrists would come. When we look at history, we see that the end-time drama plays out repeatedly on a much lesser scale. Nations come under the sway of Antichrist-type leaders until the Lord brings those leaders down. Then, the cycle repeats itself again.

In any generation, there may be several antichrists in the earth, demanding allegiance. When we prepare the church for the return of Jesus, we are preparing the church to be successful in every generation.

We can simplify preparing the church to two main tasks:

1. We present the return of Jesus as the great hope of the church and speak about Jesus in such a way that hearts long for Him and His return.

2. We prepare the church to by faithful to Jesus by resisting evil and the most wicked man in history.

When we do these two things, it strengthens the church in every generation. When we set our hope on Jesus's return, it keeps the church from deception whether we are tested by ease and comfort or suffering and distress. The coming Antichrist will bring prosperity[1] and trouble. Both are tests we must be ready for.

---

[1] See 1 Thessalonians 5:3; Revelation 18.

God uses small tribulations to bring His church to maturity before the day of big tribulation. As we study the end times the way God intended us to, it prepares us to engage in God's mission and overcome the antichrists of our generation. Overcoming the antichrists in each generation strengthens the church and prepares her to face the ultimate Antichrist.

Pursue the Knowledge of God

The primary goal of studying the end times is to grow in the knowledge of God because God reveals Himself in what He does. This includes both what He has done and what He will do. As we study what He will do, it should cause us to grow in love for Him. We see His faithfulness and His commitment to His promises. We are stunned by His patience with Israel and the nations.

We learn His emotions as we read the oracles of the prophets. The information the Bible gives us about the end of the age is important, and we want to know it. But the primary objective of any study of the end times is to grow in the knowledge of God. *When we study the end times correctly, it will cause us to love Jesus more.* And this should be our goal and our objective. This is what will allow us to trust Him even in the context of suffering.

The Study of the End-Times Is Relational and Missional

The end times can be confusing if they are treated like a period of time that is disconnected from the main story of redemption. However, when we understand the key components of the story of redemption, we can plainly see the things that must be concluded before the age ends.

Understanding the overarching story of redemption through the lens of God's promises to Israel and the nations gives us a basic framework to grasp the main themes of the Bible. Once we get this framework in place, the end-time story makes more sense, and we can make more sense of the details the Bible gives us. Understanding the story of redemption in this way also helps us understand God's work in our own generation because the Bible is the only thing that makes sense of the geopolitical issues in the earth. God is just as involved in the nations now as He has ever been.

The primary point of understanding God's plan is not only to grow in knowledge. It is not merely an academic pursuit of irrelevant information. We want to understand what God has said about His plan so we can engage with it and cooperate with Him. The study of the end times is fundamentally *relational* and *missional*.

It is relational because it causes us to grow in love for Jesus. When we study the end-time drama, we discover a side of Jesus we do not see anywhere else. He becomes more tender, more majestic, and more beautiful to us.

It is missional because it gives us understanding to better partner with God in His mission. We can partner with God in His plan with very little understanding of what the Bible says about Jesus' return, but the more we understand, the better we can partner with Him and prepare for the days ahead—days of power and glory unlike anything we've ever seen.

ACKNOWLEDGEMENTS

Thank you to my wife whose labor and sacrifice make it possible for us to engage in the task the Lord has given us.

Thank you to all the teachers who have invested in my life personally or through their ministry. I cannot name everyone, but I want to highlight a few who made this book possible.

Thank you first to my father for faithfully teaching the foundations of the faith and being an example.

Thank you to Janee Hawks for being a faithful teacher of the Word and for opening doors for me to teach.

I am forever grateful for Art Katz. Art's message helped me begin to grasp the end times by encouraging me to take the prophets literally.

Thank you to Mike Bickle for your example and the investment of your life to teach what the Bible says about the return of Jesus. I'm forever grateful.

Thank you to Reggie Kelly. You are a true role model in your commitment to the prophetic Scriptures. Thank you for hours of conversation and emails that have helped shape what is expressed in this book.

Thank you to Bryan Purtle for your friendship and input on this manuscript. Your input made a significant difference in the final manuscript.

Thank you to Jason Chua for your friendship and for naming this book. Without you this book would still be stuck without a name.

Thank you to Edie Mourey for your work on this manuscript. Your efforts improved it significantly.

Samuel Whitefield's primary labor is as an intercessor in the context of night and day prayer. He is also an author and speaker. He is the director of OneKing, a ministry that helps connect the global church to God's purposes for Israel and the nations. He also serves on the senior leadership team of the International House of Prayer of Kansas City and as faculty at the International House of Prayer University.

For additional resources please visit samuelwhitefield.com.

Made in the USA
San Bernardino, CA
30 July 2018